"**A**cross the weeks, Criedne wandered through wilderness, into the duns and cooking places of the Fianna. When she told her story, their indignity was roused. They taught her to fight remorselessly and hunt unawed, to run soundlessly, to render herself invisible, to love danger, and memorize the twelve poetic forms. They united behind her until she had acquired three bands, each with nine grim-visaged warriors.

She led them to the northern reaches of her father's land. There she first made known her boiling power and tested her strength. Clashing, billowing, slashing and cutting, the Fianna of Criedne pillaged Conall Blackfoot's territory. They built a cairn to mark the sacking of villages and farms. They left the women and children with a message for Conall to return the birthright of Criedne's sons, lest all his people and property be devastated. . . .

Nothing could stop her. Criedne Banfennid won every skirmish, every battle, raided every mile of Conall's kingdom, rumbled and rattled across the land with her band of three times nine and every rock she struck with her sword burst into raging flame."

—from *Banfennid*

Jennifer Heath was born in Australia and raised in Latin America by an Irish mother who regaled her with Irish folk tales. But it wasn't until Heath met her first husband, a professor of Nordic folklore, that she began to seriously study Celtic literature in search of stories of powerful women—the result is *On the Edge of Dream*. A person of wide-ranging talents and interests, Heath is also America's foremost expert on the subject of black velvet paintings and the author of *Black Velvet: The Art We Love to Hate* as well as a novel about the recent war in Afghanistan, *A House White with Sorrow.*

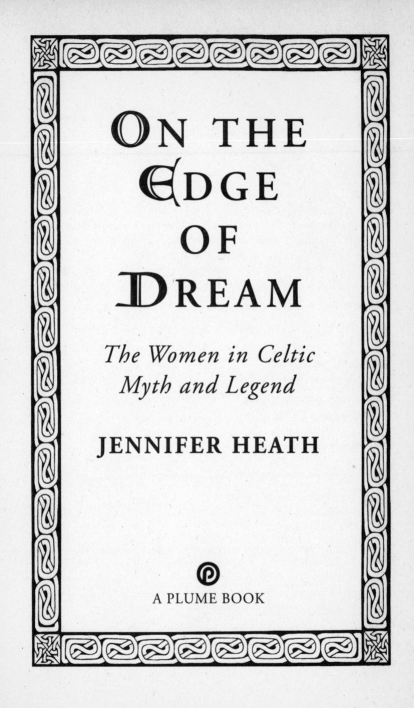

ON THE EDGE OF DREAM

The Women in Celtic Myth and Legend

JENNIFER HEATH

A PLUME BOOK

PLUME

Published by the Penguin Group

Penguin Putnam Inc., 375 Hudson Street, New York, New York 10014, U.S.A.

Penguin Books Ltd, 27 Wrights Lane, London W8 5TZ, England

Penguin Books Australia Ltd, Ringwood, Victoria, Australia

Penguin Books Canada Ltd, 10 Alcorn Avenue, Toronto, Ontario, Canada M4V 3B2

Penguin Books (N.Z.) Ltd, 182–190 Wairau Road, Auckland 10, New Zealand

Penguin Books Ltd, Registered Offices: Harmondsworth, Middlesex, England

First published by Plume, an imprint of Dutton Signet, a member of Penguin
Putnam Inc.

First Printing, March, 1998

10 9 8 7 6 5 4 3 2 1

 REGISTERED TRADEMARK—MARCA REGISTRADA

Library of Congress Cataloging-in-Publication Data is available.

Printed in the United States of America

Set in Adobe Garamond

Designed by Eve L. Kirch

BOOKS ARE AVAILABLE AT QUANTITY DISCOUNTS WHEN USED TO PROMOTE PRODUCTS
OR SERVICES. FOR INFORMATION PLEASE WRITE TO PREMIUM MARKETING DIVISION,
PENGUIN PUTNAM INC., 375 HUDSON STREET, NEW YORK, NEW YORK 10014.

In memory of my mother, Genevieve, who knew what it was to
"go to faery"—and for my godmother, Clara Redmond,
who took up where my mother left off . . .
And for Matthew and Sarah,
Sierra and Jack

CONTENTS

INTRODUCTION

This book was written in honor of my mother, who knew what it was to "go to faery," and who, with her songs, her tales, her wit, her mercurial temperament and wild fancies, taught me to go there, too.

Many of these tales—or variations of them—were told to me at the dinner table, during car rides and long train trips, in the garden (where faeries bathed in dew and set up housekeeping in the hollyhocks) and always at bedtime. Characters who occupy this book—Oisin, Niamh, Fionn, Sadb, CuChulainn, Emer, Medb—occupied my dreams and my play.

Stories were handed down to my mother from hers. But my mother, who was well educated, whereas hers was barely literate, also loved to read Celtic myth and history. Thus, the stories she told me came not only from oral tradition but from collections by William Butler Yeats and Lady Augusta Gregory, from Padraic Colum, Charles Squire and Michael Comyn. She wove the written and the oral with the rich skeins of her imagination into a brilliant tapestry of enchantment. Born in California but an Irish patriot to the end, my mother set my revolutionary heart ablaze with high-charged epics of the nationalist heroes—Wolfe Tone, Walter Devereux, the Countess Markieviez, Michael Collins—and she wept over the continuing Troubles in Northern Ireland. When I adapted "Macha," the first story in this volume, I thought of the "Pangs of Ulster" as additionally meaningful today, a curse that has spanned the centuries.

My grandmother was born in Ireland. She was over forty when she bore my mother, the last of her eight children. She was a singer, from a nation of singers and, I'm told, she sang "pure-throated as a cherub" even into quavering old age. I heard only echoes of this magnificent voice, when my mother invoked spells and chants of the Otherworld or crooned lullabies that were never soft, sticky cradle tunes but rowdy sea chanties, bawdy love ballads or baleful political laments.

My ancestors were part of the massive Irish diaspora that started in the eighteenth century and spread around the world, especially to Australia, Canada and the United States. These were not exuberant, squalling resettlements like the migrations of the ancient Celts, who were said to have moved east to west seeking the "home of the Sun." The Irish emigrations were sorrowful, forced departures, exiles preceded by wakes for living folk who would likely never see their families again or the stolen land they loved, who faced uncertain futures fraught with prejudice. The Ireland from which my great-grandparents fled in the nineteenth century was sad, depleted and wretched, harrowed by bloody British tyranny, evictions, overpopulation, desperate poverty and the Hunger.

Once upon a time, Ireland was empty and pristine, the last chunk of unpeopled territory in Europe. Wild horses and giant deer, which had crossed the land bridge between Ireland and Scotland, roamed the fecund, boggy meadows left by a retreating ice sheet. Many millennia later, according to Celtic mythology, horses and deer spoke and changed from animal to human at the breath of a *fith-fath*.

The forests grew, the Irish elk disappeared. The sea rose to separate Ireland from the rest of the world. Into this wooded, green place, a Mesolithic people drifted, probably from Britain and Scandinavia. They were small, dark folk who hunted and gathered on the fertile land, undisturbed for three thousand years. They left no traces of civilization. Their remains exist only in bones, rubbish heaps and campfires.

Were they the Fir Bolg of legend, a pre-Celtic people said to have been vanquished to the Aran Islands? Or were these Mesolithics transformed into the mythic Fomorii, demonic behemoths whose King Balor's single eye emitted deadly vapors whenever he aimed it at an enemy?

There are varying histories of pagan Ireland. The twelfth-century *Lebor Gabala*, or *Book of Invasions*, and the *Dinnshenchas*, the *History of Places*—compiled by monks from oral tradition across six hundred years—describe the settlement of the land through racial memory and mythology. The monks also preserved Irish history in two great mythological cycles: the Ulster (Red Branch) of the *Táin Bó Cuailnge*, or *Cattle Raid of Cooley*, which marks the Heroic Age; and the Fionn (Ossianic) Cycle, tales of Fionn mac Cumhall and the Fianna.

In our century, the prehistory of Ireland and the Celts has been pieced together by archeologists, paleontologists, linguists, folklorists, mythographers and scholars. Interpretations are constantly being revised in the wake of new discoveries.

Perhaps the Neolithic people who arrived on Ireland's shores around 3700 B.C.—possibly from the Mediterranean—were the divine race of the Tuatha De Danann, introduced in the *Book of Invasions*. In mythico-history, the Tribes of the goddess Danu-Ana conquered the Fir Bolg and the Fomorii. At any rate, they were agriculturists who cleared and tilled the land, tamed wild animals and left their spiritual mark with cairns and standing stones. Their elaborate megaliths were carved in spirals, braids and diamonds, in abstract, geometric, cosmic patterns. They traded gold, bronze, pottery and beads with the rest of Europe.

Theirs are the older gods of the Irish pantheon, headed by the Daghda, a vulgar, voracious deity, frequently the butt of jokes. The ancients treated their gods with humor and ridicule, as well as reverence, for human and divine behavior were interchangeable. The Daghda carried a colossal club, sometimes confused with his outsize phallus. His name is actually a title, meaning "the Good," not a moral reference, but "good" meaning competent. The Daghda was associated with magic and abundance, which he derived from his inexhaustible cauldron. As a god of fertility, he mated with the mother goddess Boane, the spirit of the river Boyne, and with the Morrigna (or Morrigan), goddess of destruction, thus assuring the safety of his people. He is the father of Brigit, triple goddess of poetry, childbirth and crafts.

The Celts were the last prehistoric arrivals on the Emerald Isle. They brought a new crop of gods, chief of whom was Lugh, the Shining One, a solar hero whose festival is Lughnasad, on August 1, established in tribute to his foster mother. His

Welsh equivalent is Lleu Llaw Gyffes. The cities of Carlisle, England (Luguvallium), and Lyon, France (Lugdunum), were named for him.

Archeological evidence indicates that the Celts dribbled into Ireland, tribe by tribe, in a slow migration from 2100 B.C. to 1300 B.C. But according to the *Book of Invasions,* the Celts swept onto the island all at once as the Sons of Mil. These nine brothers came with thirty ships and the Tuatha De Danann sent a mighty wind to drown them. Only four of Mil's sons survived. As the youngest, the poet-druid Amergin, set his right foot upon the beach, he sang a song of creation, which sealed the Milesians forever to the land:

> *I am an estuary into the sea.*
> *I am a wave of the ocean.*
> *I am a powerful ox.*
> *I am a hawk on a cliff.*
> *I am a dewdrop in the sun. . . .*

The Tuatha De Danann could not withstand the Sons of Mil. Amergin divided Ireland, giving the upper world to his brothers and the Otherworld—under earth and sea and the isles beyond the horizon—to the Tuatha De, who lived magnificently in the mounds, the magical *Sidhe.* They mingled with mortals, as lovers, friends and tormentors. Two countries in one: the faery lands of eternal youth and feasting, cheek by jowl with the hardscrabble, ordinary world of mortals with its grief, corruption and death.

Over the centuries, in concert with the oppression of Ireland by the British—which began in the twelfth century when Pope Adrian IV gave Ireland to Plantagenet Henry II—the Tuatha

De Danann have mostly shrunk to elves and gnomes, leprechauns and Little People. Although the faeries are ever alive in the Celtic mind, they have been impoverished. Once upon a time, they were shimmering, regal deities, and their relationship with humans was both spiritually and pragmatically symbiotic. Periodically, humans immigrated to faery lands, where time stopped. Like Oisin—son of Fionn and the last pagan Irishman—they discovered, upon returning and touching mortal ground, that they were doomed to sudden old age and ashes.

The Tuatha De Danann meandered back and forth between Ireland and Wales, assuming different aspects and shifting slightly to suit the cultural and mythological climates. Thus the Irish sea god Manannann mac Lir is also the Welsh Manawydan ap Llyr and the Welsh horse goddess Rhiannon becomes the Irish sea queen, Fand. In both traditions, Rhiannon/Fand is the sea king's wife.

The Breton tale of Melusine, which I have titled "Mala Lucina (The Evil Midwife)," was put to paper in A.D. 1380 by Jehan d'Arras to please his patrons and is thus erroneously believed by some to be historical. The tale may have originated in Ireland, but whatever its source, the action travels around the Celtic world from Brittany to Scotland to the Blessed Isle of Women (Avalon) and back again to France.

Celts originated on the plains of central Asia. The activities of the Heroic Age, as recorded in the Ulster Cycle, recall the

Hindu *Mahabarata.* The Song of Amergin in the *Book of Invasions* brings to mind Sri Krishna's chant in the *Bhagavad-Gita.* The mother goddess Danu-Ana is far older than Ireland—in Greece she was Danae; in Russia, Dennitsa. She lent her name to the river Danube, and in India she was known as "Waters of Heaven," the mother of the Vedic gods.

Around 3000 B.C., proto-Celts domesticated the horse and began their movement west. They were an adventurous, migratory, bellicose people. The Greek Herodotus called them *keltoi* and labeled them—as he did the Romans—"barbarians." Unlike the Romans, the individualistic Celts were never given to imperial central government, though they came to dominate vast territories. Their governing bodies were the *tuath,* the tribes, and within the extended family they formed stringent social hierarchies and sophisticated codes of law.

Religious "orders" were divided into *druidh, filidh* and *baird.* The druids were arbitrators and judges, the "high priests" whose rigorous education could take as long as twenty years and included memorizing (never committing to writing) poetry and oral traditions, astronomy, geography, medicine, philosophy, law, sacrifice and divination.

The worship of female deities was tantamount. The mother goddess in all her forms was the source and flow of birth, death, truth and inspiration. In general, Celtic goddesses ruled Earth, animals and the mysteries, while male deities were tribal, involved in human activities.

Although Celtic women perform druidic/shamanistic functions as prophets, healers and sorcerers in the texts, few are actually called "druid," a fault perhaps of biased chroniclers and translators.

Nevertheless, there are some women to whom the honor is

granted. Fionn mac Cumhall's grandmother, Bodhmall, is described both as a "druidess" and a *fennid,* an outlaw. To rescue the infant Fionn from the enemies of his dead father, in some versions, Bodhmall changes into a crane, a shapeshifting skill of druids. She endows Fionn with a magical crane-skin bag, akin to a Native American medicine bundle, which can usually only be conferred from master to pupil.

Bodhmall rears the boy in a treehouse in the wilderness, sometimes with only a hound for company, sometimes with another adult female, but always among supernatural forces and isolated from the prosaic occupations of the *tuath.* She shows him the arts of survival and toughens the boy with long, arduous physical training. Like any wise spiritual mentor, when his time comes, she sends Fionn on to his own quest, to new levels of learning with new teachers.

The *filidh* were scholars and poets. Their satire—the poet's most powerful weapon—could blemish or kill an enemy. They memorized genealogies and heroic tales and were responsible for the survival of Irish mythology into the Christian era, when the Latin alphabet freed them to write. Until the advent of Christianity, *ogham* was the only Celtic writing, a system that involved horizontal notches and strokes on stone or wood and that was used largely for grave markers.

It was a woman, Creirwyn, daughter of the Welsh mother goddess Cerridwen, who discovered the *ogham* when the letter-names were presented to her as a riddle by Ogma Sunface, a god equated with the Roman Hercules. Creirwyn is called (as are many) "the most beautiful girl in the world." It's possible that in this case, "beautiful" refers not only to appearance, but also to accomplishment. It may be that Creirwyn was *filidh,* skilled in verse, prophecy and solving conundrums.

Women were *filidh* in the pagan era and were admitted to the bardic schools in early Christian Ireland. Would they not, then, have documented the ancient stories, illuminated books and composed poetry along with the monks? Could they not have had an equal hand in the creation of, say, the glorious *Book of Kells*?

The ancient *filidh* schools continued in Ireland far into the Christian era, but were suppressed in the sixteenth century by the English King Henry VIII.

Celts prized eloquence as much as physical courage. Words and their figurative use have always been magic, and essential to the Celts. Language, even playful language, was hallowed and mystical, a ritual, a way of moving through spiritual space and making things happen or answers appear.

Celts loved riddles and used them as games, metaphysical communications and even love vows, as illustrated in the courtship of CuChulainn and Emer. Not surprisingly, women are said to have excelled at riddles, and women made much of furious "word battles," whereby—usually collectively—they beat their chests, pulled at their breasts (perhaps even "mooned" their opponents) and hurled shaming, damning speech. These confrontations, and the long, feasting nights Celts spent reciting verse around the banquet halls, must have resembled today's poetry slams.

In today's vernacular, the word "bard" has come to stand for any poet. The Celtic *baird* were "court poets," singers of eulogies and praises, who presided over ceremonies and Otherworldly feasts. They reported noble deeds like versifying journalists.

Celts venerated all natural phenomena, from thunder and lightning to birdsong and the green grass growing. The *I am* by which they lived in unison with Nature. Their religion harmonized with earth, moon, sea, sun, stars, seasons and animals. Worship took place among trees. The French cathedral of Chartres was built in an oak grove, where once the Celts celebrated their mysteries. The stories of Rhiannon and Macha, the antlered images of the god Cernunnos on altars and vessels, and the tale of Sadb—all hint at horse and deer cults. There is no known Celtic creation myth, so I conjured one in "The Cailleach (Old Woman)" from bits and pieces of lore about the Daghda, Boane and the Old Woman of Bera and theories about the identity of carved images of "Sheela-na-gig," who displays her genitals on church walls and lintels and is sometimes described as the "Kali of the Celts."

The proto-Celts traversed Europe, invading, raiding and assimilating in Gaul, Iberia, Italy, Hungary, Greece, Turkey, North Africa and Britain. During the Iron Age, they occupied half of Western Europe, a period called the La Tène, the "free" Celtic era before the expansion of the Roman Empire. Celts are not one "race" but a blend of many peoples linked by language and religion. Today, Celtic countries are defined as those where a Celtic language is spoken: Ireland, Wales, Brittany, the Isle of Man and Scotland. For this reason—and because I am fascinated by folklore and mythology of any stripe—I ventured a bit beyond Irish mythology, the richest source, into other Celtic realms. "Rhiannon," "Cerridwen" and "Blodeuwedd" are Welsh, the first and third tales having been taken from the *Four Branches of the Mabinogion*.

Unfortunately, the *Mabinogion*—written down in the eleventh century A.D. and one of the few remaining Welsh texts—has been reshaped and contaminated by a slew of ethical agendas beyond the original. Whoever tampered with the

Mabinogion was not blessed with the whimsical mind of Irish monks, and turned it into something of a prim children's book. The wisdom and irony of Irish myths are here dulcified and minimized, with women coming out the losers. For example, in the story of Blodeuwedd, the rebellious flower maiden is obviously the victim of Gwydyon and Math's Pygmalionism, but in the *Mabinogion* she is blamed much like the biblical Eve.

While Celts were savage and battle-loving (fearless, for they believed in immortality through reincarnation and thought death was merely a quick bridge into the next life), they were also splendidly resourceful, imaginative and artistic. Celtic music and poetry were unparalleled throughout Europe. They were goldsmiths and engravers, weavers and dyers. They practiced enameling and glassmaking. They invented the wheel plough, the scythe and trousers. The blacksmith was revered. Their weaponry was unrivaled until the appearance of the Roman legions, who were less exquisitely armed but more organized.

Observers described the ancient Celts as "hospitable," "high-spirited," "childlike" and "never evil of character." That spontaneity and ingenuity led to their downfall.

The Celts adored decoration on their goods and ornamented their persons with lavish jewelry, often as not made of gold.

They wore bright colors and tartans, and fastened their cloaks and shirts with elaborate brooches. Men wore leather belts with intricately wrought clasps and women bound their gowns with bronze girdle chains.

Doubtless women also wore trousers when they wanted, for, although Celts loved luxury, feasting and drinking, they were a practical, athletic, hard-working people.

To be fat was unacceptable. Celts were meticulous in their

grooming and proud in their bearing. Celtic women used mirrors, tweezers and makeup. The Roman poet Propertius chastised his mistress for painting herself "like a Celt."

Greek and Roman travelers inevitably described the Celts as "tall" and "fair" (though, of course, Celtic people are now and always have been entirely diverse in stature and coloring).

Considering that the Roman army averaged less than 5 feet in height, these people—who often cleared 6 feet—must indeed have seemed like giants. The Roman Ammianus Marvellius, visiting Gaul in the fourth century A.D., was awed by the "tall, blue-eyed, singularly beautiful" women. The British Iceni queen Boudicca, who led the most ferocious revolt ever against the Roman army around A.D. 60, was said to have been "huge of frame with masses of bright red hair that fell to her knees."

Women and men wore their hair long, pulled it back from their faces and washed it in lime, which bleached and thickened it to look, Caesar wrote, "like horses' manes." The lime washes may have had the effect of "dreading" the hair. In battle, Celts spiked it like fright wigs. Naked, wearing only gold torcs around their necks, shrieking, taunting, hair standing on end and, in the case of the Britons, their bodies painted blue with woad, they must have been a terrifying sight to oncoming Roman troops.

Homes were round and made of timber and wicker. Cooking was done in huge cauldrons hung from crossbeams that led to a smoke hole. In Celtic myth, the cauldron, source of sustenance, is venerated. There are cauldrons of rebirth and reincarnation, cauldrons of plenty and regeneration, such as the Daghda's, though they are usually kept in the care of Otherworldly women. Later, in Arthurian legends, these abundant cauldrons converge into the Holy Grail.

Women's daily life was a matter of "chop wood/carry water." They hand-milled flour, wove fine cloth from the fleece of their sheep and plowed the fields (a good reason to wear pants!). Because Celtic society was divided into "noble, free and *un*free," privileged women had slaves and servants. And while children were fostered—sent to be reared by friends and allies, the girls until they were fourteen, the boys until they were seventeen— the Greek geographer Strabo wrote that Celtic women were notably loving, attentive mothers.

Irish mythology and oral history, put to parchment by monks while the rest of Europe languished in the so-called Dark Ages, does not spell out as clearly as it might the high place of women in pre- and early Christian Celtic society. That is not its job. Numerous earthly women have supreme authority in Irish and Welsh texts, not to speak of the supremacy of Otherworld queens. The *Sidhe* is frequently called "The Land of Women," indicating a pre-Celtic, pre-Milesian matriarchal culture.

The Victorians—who collected folklore, translated the Gaelic texts and restructured them for popular audiences during the Irish Renaissance—tended to focus on nobility, nostalgia and romantic symbols of an illustrious Irish past, slighting "lesser" female characters in favor of glamorous ones. A seemingly endless stream of poems, plays and stories recounted the adventures of the marvelous, promiscuous and blatantly aggressive Queen Medb, who enjoyed offering "the friendship of her thighs" (a foil to Queen Victoria and the corseted mores of the day?), and the tragic romance of Deirdre of the Sorrows. But of Criedne, who suffered incest, or Mis, who is coaxed out of her awkward, adolescent "wolfgirl" phase through sexual initiation, we hear very little except in obscure scholarly papers.

We know from sources such as Julius Caesar—who invaded Britain in 54 B.C. and who completed his conquest of Gaul by 51 B.C. but never got to Ireland—that Celtic women were at liberty to design their own lives, within the confines of tight social strata. Celtic social structure was less misogynist than classist, and was not, at the time of the Romans, matriarchal, though there was matrilineal succession. Men headed the *tuath,* yet the complex laws were predicated on equality, providing for women's independence, ascendancy and choice, much to Caesar's horror. Roman women were property and playthings. Celtic women were integrated in political and religious life. In the lists of great lawyers of pagan Ireland, there are women's names.

In Celtic society, cattle equaled wealth and women owned herds. It is in order to increase her fortune over and above her husband's that Queen Medb of Connacht makes war on Ulster in the *Táin.* Celts considered women morally superior—which may account for the apparently infantile behavior of heroes such as CuChulainn. The tale of Macha, wherein men are cursed to experience the defenseless pain of labor without the fulfillment of birth, can be viewed as a morality tale against the mistreatment of women.

Some contemporary scholars speculate that the stories of Fionn mac Cumhall and the Fianna, in the Ossianic Cycle, are, in fact, coming-of-age tales. To become a *fennid*—an outlaw, as it was then defined—was rather like participating in a walkabout, or vision quest, or spending time in a ferocious (and hallucinogenic) Outward Bound program. Both men and women left the *tuath* for *fennidecht,* to live in the wild, but most eventually returned to society. Fionn never left *fennidecht.* His home was the natural world and women were his link to human society or the world beyond. His adventures and those of his close companions range in and out of the supernatural. Thus he remains caught on the threshold between childhood and adulthood. Little is detailed in popular literature of the women who became *banfennid*. What stories exist, such as the tales of Criedne and Nessa, and even Mis, bear exploring and repeating.

Celtic women went to war and frequently trained young warriors. The Ulster hero CuChulainn learned skill at arms and his famous salmon leap from Scatach the Shadowy One at her "military academy" on Alba. Boane was called the "nurse of heroes." King Conchobar's daughter was also his battle-charioteer.

In battle, women led the way onto the field, naked furies, marching ahead of the men, screaming, howling, banging war clappers and making word battles, brandishing torches in a fearsome ritual reenactment of the Morrigna, the war goddesses casting the spell of victory.

And when her man was down, the Celtic woman was likely to jump into the fray and fight in his place.

Marriage among Celts was not inviolable, as it became with Christianity. Marriage was secular, not religious. Nor did married women give up their property or any rights—as did Roman women, who had few to begin with. Marriage in Celtic society was a free union that could be broken. Celts were lusty and not as squeamish as many late nineteenth- and early twentieth-century mythographers and folklorists, who, with few exceptions and many euphemisms, expurgated the "naughty bits." Pre-Christian Celts had few sexual taboos, took their pleasure as they liked, and accepted open homosexuality. Aristotle declared that Celtic men "are inclined to let themselves be dominated by the women; this is not an unusual tendency among energetic warrior races. Apart," he added, "from the Celts who respect manly love quite openly."

Women were as often sexual initiators as men. In that spirit, believing that sexual activity is integral to these tales, I have included it—or, more likely, reinstated it. Among the themes in Celtic mythology is woman-as-teacher, whose appearance transforms the landscape and the male universe. Through sexual relations, she initiates men and brings harmony, fertility and wholeness. An interesting exception is "The Romance of Mis and Dubh Ruis," in which the male becomes the healer.

When St. Patrick went to Ireland in the fifth century A.D., followed by the monks who established the monasteries where Irish literature and art flourished, a kind of druidic Christianity took root, a sensual, spiritual partnership between Christ (another solar hero) and Nature, happily insulated for centuries from papal politics. St. Patrick was said to have conjured the *fith-fath* to transform himself into a deer. In this "golden age" of Christianity, men and women cohabited freely in Irish monasteries.

Much of the greatest Irish poetry springs from the "wailing women," who in some places still improvise narrative verse in their keening laments for the dead. The "waulking" songs— whereby women (and some men) tell stories and gossip in extemporaneous verse while they work at weaving—might also be sources for Celtic poetry and storytelling. In *On the Edge of*

Dream I have tried to be true to these forms by employing, as much as possible, a prose chant style. I have also integrated lines of Celtic poems (from antiquity to Yeats) directly into the texts, because I love the cadences and images.

I am a fabler, not a professional scholar, yet it seems to me that the powerful role and influence of Celtic women throughout the ages as creators and guardians of oral tradition, and especially as women who once lived as equals to men, has been undermined. It is to that undermining that I have, in part, addressed these tales and retold them to fulfill a female point of view. And after all, it is from the female line that I first received them.

Tales naturally change and change and again change with the telling. The changes—as I learned at my mother's knee—are bound not only to the imagination of the teller but to the times. Sagas and mythologies are my primary sources, but I have also integrated folktales in which the same characters continue on to further, "unofficial" adventures (rather like Christ strolling around Sicily, Norway or New Mexico, making miracles and chatting with his disciples). The foundation for the stories in this book was built in my childhood. The rest took years of research. Each tale is followed by a brief list of collections, poets and scholars to whom I am indebted and whose names can be found in the card catalogues of most libraries by anyone who wishes to shuffle back to the sources.

I have fashioned some of these stories from the barest fragments, and here and there I've woven scraps together. As a fiction writer, I've revisioned and reshaped them all in my own way, fleshed them out with my own idiosyncrasies, biases and desires, and in the process, I have tried to discover each story's feminist secret, its "key." Although I like to think that they would please my mother and grandmother, I have retold them to satisfy my own heart. I hope they satisfy the reader's.

Jennifer Heath
Boulder, Colorado

Though now in her old age, in her young age
She had been beautiful in that old way
That's all but gone; for the proud heart is gone,
And the fool heart of the counting-house fears all
But soft beauty and indolent desire.
She could have called over the rim of the world
Whatever woman's lover had hit her fancy,
And yet had been great-bodied and great-limbed,
Fashioned to be the mother of strong children;
And she'd had lucky eyes and a high heart,
And wisdom that caught fire like the dried flax,
At need, and made her beautiful and fierce,
Sudden and laughing.

—W. B. Yeats
"The Old Age of Queen Maeve"

Macha

Stand out, maids and wives!
Look to the earth. The trees are ablaze.
Alas for the scorched and blighted land!
Alas for the creatures who have lost their dens!
Alas for the young who long for their brothers!
Alas for the babes who cry for their fathers!
Alas for the mothers whose sons will not attend their deathbeds!
Alas for the widows alone on their cots!

Women keened on the battlefield. The sky was black with birds. A thousand crows hovered above the reddened ground where men lay maimed and dying and women swayed and beat their chests and clapped their palms and ripped their hair and keened.

Dismal! O dismal!
Without a soft bed.
A cold, frosty dwelling.
O harsh and hard is death!

And my own dear man, so stubborn in battle.
The bright heart.

Hall without fire, without bed.
I weep and then I'll be silent awhile.

The crows circled. The infinite flap of their wings swooped through the keening women's cloaks and they shuddered. The crows floated on the heat of lamentations, hot current drifted upward from the bloodied Ulster ground.

No flame.
No hard sword to warm my bed.
Long! Long! O dreadful yearning!
You are shapeless, your shield in the grave, and I
  am loveless, oh!

The hall is grim tonight!
Crow has swallowed her gory drink.
Crow wallows in the blood of men, greedy for the flesh I love,
  while I, a heavy grief upon me, cling to my beloved.

My brothers grew like hazel saplings.
One by one, they pass away.
Woe, woe is me that I am still alive!

Closer they dropped and tighter and tighter their crow ranks. They skimmed the smoldering trees. They merged. Where there had been a thousand crows, three ladies touched the ground.

The war-weavers. The Morrigna.

And the first to land was the Phantom Queen. Now her cloudy dress was tranquil. Hours before, it was the color of thunder. Its spin and huff and twirl and squall had nourished and agitated petty squabbles. She was phantom, for few ever remembered why or how the battles began.

Frenzy landed on the shoulders of a wailing woman. So airy, the woman did not notice. The battle fury, the rage Frenzy had choreographed, the killing fear in the killing field, was done. Now she bayed with the women and she stirred their alases and woes.

Macha hovered above the scene. She let her crow's coat melt only gradually away. She had cast charms to strengthen her favorite warriors in battle. Now she snickered and cawed and her screams loosened the mortal hold of the dead.

The Phantom Queen glided across the field. She grasped the dangling thread of a widow's hood and yanked it gently. She split the thread in three. Frenzy hopped from her perch on the wailing woman's shoulders and she took the third. Trilling and humming like three flutes, they wove a fragile web from the mourning cloak around the battleground, and the brown threads gleamed gold with dew and dawn and peace at last beginning.

The Phantom Queen turned to the brackish river. She straddled the ford to receive the spirits of the slain in her womb and she washed their bloody wounds and she slapped their bloody linens clean across her knees.

Frenzy picked at bones and flesh and guts, devoured eyes and lips from staked heads and sipped from pools of blood, and when she had her fill she flew away.

Macha soothed and repaired the packed, reddened earth with her soles and palms, and wherever she scratched and stroked, heather and broom and flax and all beauty returned.

The keening women dragged home their men's remains.

Their ululations trailed across the heath, and only three dusty and dazed warriors were left to stumble home behind them.

Eternal sea, mother and tomb.
The war-weaver becomes the lover.
Death, the giver of life.
Now the destroyer's second task:
She rushes toward creation.

Macha ran to a hill that overlooked the sea. She ran across the winter hill and she ran like racing wind and racing laughter and racing horses and no one could ever outrace her and she ran until she reached a valley where there was a house, the hold of a chieftain, a widower with three small, lonely boys.

Macha knocked on the door of the chieftain's house, and though he feared the risen dead on this Samhain day, he welcomed her. He could not take his eyes from her comely face, her violet hair that poured along her back like black cream and in which one violet-black feather still clung.

Crunnchu could not take his eyes from Macha's bird-boned figure. He could not leave whatever room she was in.

Macha spoke no word and set about to right his shabby rooms. His wealth was gone, his servants disappeared. The richness of his land had been plunged into ravenous warriors' mouths. His stores were empty. His motherless children were hungry.

She stoked the fire. She righted his rooms. She piled the table with warm, good foods. The children rubbed their bellies, and when they had eaten every bite she kissed them and tucked them in their beds and their sleep was sound. They slept soundly and Crunnchu thanked her. She pointed her chin toward his bedcloset. He obeyed and she followed him.

He lay on his cot and he watched her. She turned three circles to the right and right again and again right and she blessed the house. She stripped her frock and she entered his bed.

Crunnchu stroked her neck. He rubbed his beard on her breasts. She turned her back to him and she opened her legs. He lay softly on her spine and he wrapped his thighs around her buttocks and folded his arms around her waist and cupped her downy mound and gently squeezed her birdlike bones. She spoke not a word, but cooed and gurgled deep within her throat.

Wordless Macha attended Crunnchu's bed and Crunnchu's house. None resented her silence. Her loving smiles healed the ruin.

She lovingly planted and harvested ruined gardens and orchards. She filled Crunnchu's storehouses to overflowing. She cooked and weaved. She cut the peat and chopped the kindling. She ran up the hill and down to the sea to gather Crunnchu's scattered flocks, and none could outwork nor outrun her, not even the strongest, fastest horses, though they, and even the children, tried in playful races to defeat her.

Every night, Macha turned three circles right and right again and again right, and day by day they prospered till one by one Crunnchu's retinue returned.

At midsummer, Macha's belly was fat and prosperous and kicking. Crunnchu prepared to attend the Lughnasad assembly of the high king and all the Ulstermen.

Crunnchu promised to be home soon. Macha clung to him and she spoke the first words she had ever spoken to Crunnchu.

Do not boast about me, she said.

7

Crunnchu cocked his bearded jaw as if he had only imagined he'd heard that gentle voice.

You would be difficult to keep a secret, he said as if he were answering a breeze. Crunnchu embraced Macha and his children and he departed.

Woe the bright heart dimmed with pride!
Boneless and shapeless his desires.
He tumbles toward the downward spiral.
Alas creation wears the skin of doom!
Harsh and hard the bed and cold the hall.

Mead and milk and music. Courts and councils and marriage bargains. Cakes and cattle and pigs and pies and sheep and dances and games. Chieftains and slaves and poets and druids and warriors crowded the Ulster Assembly and gathered around a track where highbred horses raced.

Beautiful horses. Flying manes, smooth flanks, grace and speed and sheen and shine. Crunnchu had brought no horses to race that day and he was dazzled and jealous. He turned to the man beside him.

My wife is faster than the high king's favorite mount. She can outrun the finest stallions that pull his lightest chariots, Crunnchu said. Ambition drove the promise, her kindness, and the peace she brought, from his memory. She had spoken so softly, he could let himself forget.

And with every race, Crunnchu boasted to the man beside him until word at last reached the high king. The high king called for Crunnchu.

Are you merely a braggart? he asked.

But Crunnchu insisted his wife could outrun any creature alive.

Crunnchu insisted and the high king sent a messenger to summon Macha to the race.

Macha rubbed her kicking belly to show the messenger how soon her time was to come. She shook her violet hair and the violet-black feather slapped her chin and she patted the plump cheeks of Crunnchu's three motherless boys and she shook her head again.

Your husband will be shamed and killed if you do not appear, the messenger said.

Macha kissed the children farewell. She dragged her feet behind the messenger. He lifted her onto his pony and he carried her to the Ulster Assembly.

She spoke not a word and her eyes sought Crunnchu. From a distance, Crunnchu smiled encouragement. He wagered with chieftains and poets and druids and warriors. He wagered his wife would outrun the high king's finest horses. Men shouted and laughed and cheered and jeered. They mocked Macha's heavy waist. Macha's eyes begged them to stop and none returned her gaze.

Her pleading gaze was lost in the merriment. Macha quivered at the starting line. Two horses hitched to the king's lightest chariot waited beside her and they foamed and scraped their hooves in the dust. Macha's back was bowed with the weight in her belly. The horses were lean and restless.

The high king shouted. Macha felt the crack of a stick across her rump.

Macha ran. Neck and neck with the horses. They galloped so hard and so close, the whistle of the charioteer's whip tangled with Macha's violet hair. She thrust her bucking belly forward. She ran and ran and her legs lengthened. The lathered horses leaped ahead. Macha strained on and on, her gait quickened

9

and her arms pumped like wings. Pushing and panting, she ran and the blue veins popped on her belly. The horses snorted and dropped back. Macha limped across the finish line and she collapsed. The birthwaters burst in her belly and flushed between her thighs.

Macha rolled on the ground in birthwater and she wept without words and the Ulstermen chattered in awe above her. Crunnchu cowered in the crowd. Macha screamed. The load in her belly contracted. She groaned and grunted, and twins, a son and a daughter, slid out along her wet and bird-boned legs.

The babies howled. Macha's sight was blinded by sweat and she gasped and wheezed and spoke a second time.

Hear my curse, cruel bearded men of Ulster! You who would not help me! All you who hear my screams, you, who do not honor me! I curse you! For nine generations, in times of greatest peril, when enemies are at your door, you bearded men of Ulster will writhe, unprotected, uncomforted, for five long days, with stinging belly cramp and shooting back pain, legs spread helplessly, as weak as women in childbirth.

And Macha died.

Macha died and Crunnchu flung the winnings from his hand. Now he pushed through the crowd around his wife on the dusty track. They tried to give him his howling babies, and overhead, a flock of crows cawed and shrieked and croaked.

Two ladies in black hoods and mourning cloaks swayed and beat their chests and ripped their hair and clapped their hands and keened.

Alas the lover's peace destroyed!
Bounty she brought out of ruin.
Woe you trespassers, usurpers and breachers of faith.

Soon begin the Pangs of Ulster!
Long-lasting evil.
Woe you men without mercy!
Make ready the bed of pain and agony!
The bed that receives no life.

The Morrigna swaddled Macha's body and her twin babies. Her violet-black feather was all they left behind. Chieftains and slaves and poets and druids and warriors and the high king watched horrified as the sky grew thick and black with a thousand crows.

In Connacht, fierce, mighty Queen Medb gathered her army to take the Brown Bull of Ulster. The Phantom Queen glided through the great ranks. Her spin and huff and twirl and squall nourished petty agitations. Macha cast her charms for favorites and Frenzy raised her cry of wrath and rage and panic.

red and crimson and scarlet
scarlet and red and crimson
crimson and scarlet and red

Medb's warriors crossed the plain. They crossed the boundaries of Ulster. Ahead of the hordes, Medb's painted women waved flaming torches. They beat war drums. They bawled the curdling war songs. Medb's army marched with clatter of swords and whinnying horses and chariots and five-pronged spears and fluted shields across fields and valleys and through the forests of Ulster, and closer and closer came the great peril.

At Emain Macha, at Macha's death place, a child heard the roaring footsteps and trumpets and the crash and cries of advancing warriors and the blue sky was blackened by a thousand crows.

The child ran to warn the others. But the bearded men of Ulster were crumbling, one by one, with stinging belly cramp and shooting back pain, legs spread helplessly apart, as weak as women in childbirth.

Retold from the Irish *Táin Bó Cuailnge*.

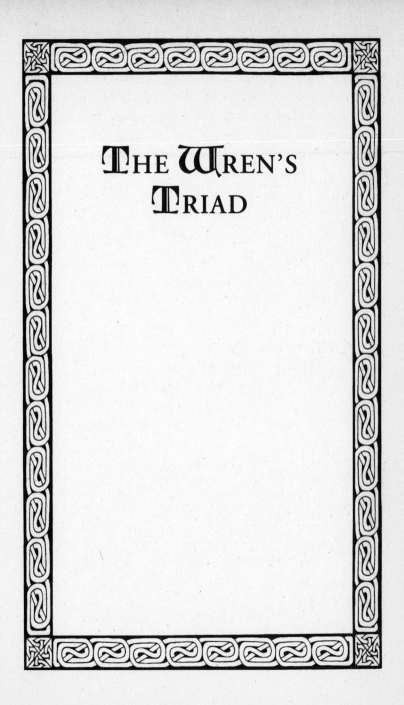

THE WREN'S TRIAD

I
Rhiannon

The White Night Mare traverses the sky from this world to the Other. She nests in the consciences of kings.

 near the Caer of Narberth, where Pwyll, Chief of Dyfed, had his court, there was a mound. Whenever a warrior sat on it, he had one of two adventures.

He might receive wounds and blows, inflicted by the invisible, beating wings of the White Night Mare.

Or he might see a great and splendid wonder. It might be the Moon kissing the Sun at noon. It might be a herd of gold and silver cattle charging along the horizon. Fish swimming in dry grasses. The skulls of a thousand ancient warlords risen to remember their victories and telling their tales all at once.

One day, when his court was assembled to break their fast, Pwyll announced that he would sit on the mound. And after a while he saw, approaching along the road, at an easy trot, a lady dressed in white garments, astride a sleek, mettlesome white mare. Three golden wrens circled her head.

Pwyll dashed from man to woman and woman to man, asking, "Who knows that lady?" But none did.

"Well, then," he barked, "find out!"

As his men moved toward the White Lady, she moved away, and however fast they rode, she kept an even distance between them and never quickened her quiet pace, though they exceeded theirs.

Each day, Pwyll sent a man to chase the woman. Perhaps it was the sweet song of her wrens which dazed the messenger, for he always returned at dusk frustrated and empty-handed.

Pwyll could not sleep. He tossed and turned. He dreamed of the White Night Mare. He dreamed of mounting the mare and making love to her. He dreamed of bathing in a broth of her milk. He dreamed he drank all her blood. He dreamed he could not harness her, though in his dreams he tried. He dreamed until, at last, he understood that only *he* could overtake the lady, who rode round and round the mound, day after day, a pure white iris of mist.

Again, he ascended the mound. With sunrise, the White Lady emerged.

He leaped onto his fastest stallion and rushed after her. She tossed her tresses, snowy waves, buoyant as apple blossoms, which coiled into the mare's white mane and tail, as if woman and horse were one. Pwyll chased her, and when he was near enough to see the glint and wink of the crescent moonstone around her neck, he called, "Hold there! Lady! Rein in!" She whispered to the mare and the mare set her ears back and they were gone.

Each morning for thirteen months, Pwyll chased the White Lady, calling her, but she did not answer, she would not wait.

Until one morning, he spoke these words: "Lady, for the sake of the man you love best, stop for me."

And she did.

He galloped fast toward her, afraid to lose her again. He pulled up beside her, but the right words he'd finally captured had been said and he seemed to have no others.

"You . . . lady . . . you . . . white . . . what is . . . your . . . errand?" he choked.

"You are my errand," she replied, and the wrens chirped in rhyme with Pwyll's pounding heart.

"I am Rhiannon," she said, "and my father, Heveydd the Old, has sought to give me a husband against my will. I will not sleep with any man I have not chosen, and I have chosen you and with you would share my wealth and my delights. What is your answer? Will you love me?"

Pwyll nodded.

"Where is your voice, brave chieftain?" she teased.

Pwyll struggled against muteness. He cleared his throat. "Love you? Does the rain bring flowers in spring?" he asked. "Do salmon swim upstream? Do the leaves turn brown in fall?"

"Not where I come from," she laughed. "Go on, my lord, you may be nearing something akin to a poem."

But Pwyll could not go on. "Yes," he said simply. "Yes. Tell me what to do."

"Wait another thirteen months," she said, and he sighed. "Then, at midnight, that rock will open into the mound. Within the mound is an orchard, and deep in the orchard, un-der the lair of the White Night Mare, you will find my father and me and Gwawl ap Clud, the man I am to wed, feasting with all our company. You will know Gwawl, for he has a clawed hand and many horses, which he spirits from your world

17

into ours on each New Year. The horses glow, but beneath their bellies are shadows. They will be tethered throughout the orchard.

"Do not come as a chieftain, Pwyll, though you must bring a company of ninety-nine men. Tell your men to hide under the horses.

"Then come alone to us as a ragged beggar. Bring your hunting horn and bring this bag." Rhiannon pulled a rough little sack from her girdle and handed it to Pwyll.

"Ask Gwawl ap Clud to fill the bag with raw flesh. The bridegroom cannot refuse a supplicant, for the day's good fortune belongs to him.

"There is no amount of meat in your world and mine that will fill this bag. When Gwawl begins to grumble, you must say that in order for the hungry bag to be satisfied, a nobleman must jump in and tread on the contents. When Gwawl does so, you must quickly turn the bag upside down and tie the strings into a knot, then blow the hunting horn so that your men will appear by your side."

Rhiannon reached across the mare and kissed Pwyll, a kiss he returned with vigor to seal his pledge.

Thirteen months later, Pwyll layered rags over his battle garb and hung his hunting horn around his neck and hooked the little bag to his belt. The chieftain and his ninety-nine men stood by the rock, which creaked open at midnight. Then, slowly, fearfully, they entered the mound. Pwyll led the way along a dark path that seemed to descend for miles, until a kind of ocean dawn unfolded and they found themselves in an orchard, where ripened fruit hung heavy as jewels from every branch and a hundred horses, dappled and chestnut and auburn, horses of every shade and shape, were tied to the trees. The horses blazed like stars and torches in sunlight, an illusive light-on-light, yet under every horse there was a patch of black shadow, where Pwyll's men hid.

Then Pwyll proceeded alone until he came to the banquet table. He begged Gwawl ap Clud for meat. He tricked Gwawl into the bag exactly as Rhiannon had instructed. He tied the strings of the bag in a tight knot. He blew his hunting horn and his men appeared at his side.

Rhiannon reared from her seat. Whinnying with anger and urgency, she told Pwyll's men that she had a game with which they must entertain the assembled company. "Kick the bag back and forth between you, like a ball," she said.

And they divided into teams and tossed and hurled the bag, dribbled, booted, trampled and punted it, and knelt upon it when it resisted.

At last, a muffled voice cried out to Heveydd the Old: "Lord, stop them! Death in a bag is no proper end for me!"

And Heveydd, who was very old indeed, for he was Lord of the Otherworld, where death never ventures, bid his daughter stop the game.

"Have you not now had sufficient vengeance for the bargain struck for you, Rhiannon? Are you not now content to have your choice of husbands?"

Rhiannon's lip curled. Her teeth glinted. She snorted, tossed her head and held up her hand to Pwyll and his men. "Father, I am done. This man Pwyll, Chief of Dyfed, is my choice. Return the marriage goods, for I am no chattel, no brood mare to be traded and haggled over. But before we release him, we must demand sureties that Gwawl ap Clud will make no claims against us."

Gwawl ap Clud promised meekly, a muffled, weak promise from within the bag. They let him go. He cursed Rhiannon, a malediction so sharp it seemed to cleave her from her white crown to her white slippers, and she trembled. Gwawl flinched at the cuts and purple bruises on his face. He rubbed his clawed hand and winced. He turned his back on Rhiannon and Pwyll, and offered farewell to Heveydd the Old. He herded his radiant horses toward his own lands.

So Rhiannon and Pwyll retired and spent the night at pleasure. In the morning, the wrens woke them and they departed from the Otherworld to Dyfed.

Many years passed before Rhiannon returned to any Otherworldly place, but never again did she set foot in the orchard within the mound.

The man of might, he rode at night
With neither sword nor fear nor light
He sought the Mare, he found the Mare,
He bound the Mare with her own hair. . . .

Pwyll and Rhiannon ruled Dyfed prosperously. On the third New Year, Rhiannon felt her birth pangs and she shut herself in her bedchamber with six women.

The baby, a boy, was born as the sun set and the people of Dyfed went about lighting the New Year fires. Rhiannon and her serving women fell asleep, worn by the long labor. Rhiannon dreamed of horses and ponies, and in her dreams she visited the White Night Mare, and in the nest lined with plumage, yew branches and scalps, she gnawed on the jawbones of bards and the knuckles of farriers.

At midnight, the women woke. The eldest went first to the cradle. Looking down, she gasped and dropped to her knees to search the floor and under the benches and chests.

"The baby! The babe!" she cried. "The child is gone!"

The other five hushed her. "Pwyll would consider it a light punishment if we were only burned or executed," said one.

"Can you guess what else he might devise for us in his rage?" said another.

They killed the pup of a staghound and laid the tiny bones beside sleeping Rhiannon and smeared the blood around her face, across her mouth and between her teeth.

At dawn, the wrens whistled an alarm. Rhiannon opened her eyes and rubbed them. She asked for the child, but they told her she had devoured it.

The White Night Mare floated like a fog around her. She shook herself awake. Did she believe she had eaten her infant? She had spent her dream ambling and capering with the one who feeds on her own farrow.

Rhiannon begged the women to tell the truth. She promised to protect them from Pwyll's wrath. But they clung to their story and told one another in whispers that it *could* have happened, it *might* have, for, after all, Rhiannon was not of this world.

Until, finally, Rhiannon grew weary of begging. She could

not be sure she had not killed the infant. She knew not the course of her own action. She stood before Pwyll and his council, silently awaiting her sentence.

"I will not kill her nor put her aside," Pwyll shouted over the loud protests of his advisors. "Rhiannon came to me as a wonder and a gift. I have given her my pledge of love and I will not part with her.

"But I will inflict a penance.

"For seven years," Pwyll said, "Rhiannon is to sit all day by the horse-mounting block at the castle gate and tell her guilty tale to every stranger who comes by. She is to say, 'Guest, come no closer. I will carry you into the court, since that is my punishment for killing my son and destroying him with my own hands and consuming him.' Then, they will mount her and she will bear each one into the caer on her back."

Pwyll, whose battles were fought with sword and spear, who had no easy companionship with words, shuffled away in gloom from Rhiannon, exhausted by his decree.

No longer was Rhiannon the proud White Lady, fleet of foot on her mettlesome mare. Now she was a beast of burden.

Pwyll watched her day after day and yearned for both her and the missing child.

In Pwyll's dreams, the White Night Mare bore Gwawl ap Clud across the sky, screaming with laughter and shaking his clawed hand. And none in Dyfed slept sound for seven years against the nightly neighs, brays, whickers and ululations in the clouds.

Tiernon, Lord of Gwent Ys Coed, across the orange mountains, possessed a fantastic mare, who foaled on every New Year. But as soon as she had foaled, the colt disappeared.

On the same day that Rhiannon's birth pangs began, Tiernon resolved to get to the bottom of this dilemma. After dark, when the people of Gwent Ys Coed lit their New Year fires, Tiernon took up arms and stationed himself in the stable.

The mare foaled as usual. And while Tiernon admired the strength and red, red color of this fresh colt, a clawed hand reached into the window and grabbed it.

Tiernon whacked the limb with his ax. It fell bleeding outside the window, still holding the colt. Wild wailing and Tiernon tumbled out of the barn, following the sound, but the thief was gone and so was the severed clawed hand. Unable to fathom what had happened or who had been there, Tiernon brought the newborn stallion into the stable. On straw, at the foot of the mare, lay a human infant wrapped in swaddling and a gold, silk blanket. Amazed, he picked up the baby and took it to his childless wife.

She caressed the silk blanket against her cheek and traced its gold threads. "He is the son of noble folk," she cooed as she rocked the baby and comforted his howls. "He will be a joy to me." She curled his downy hair with her finger and named the child Gwri White Locks.

Before Gwri's first year, he could walk and was sturdier than a well-fed three-year-old. At the end of his second year, he was strong as a six-year-old, and by the time he was four, he was able to tame and ride the red colt that had been born the same night.

Was it Rhiannon's wrens who brought word to Gwent Ys Coed that the child of Pwyll of Dyfed was missing and his queen accused and hobbled?

However the tale reached Tiernon, the moment it entered his ears, the good man knew his child Gwri was Rhiannon's own. With heavy hearts, Tiernon and his wife decided to return the boy.

They journeyed for days, traveling slowly, for they could not bear to part with the silent, strapping child, whose white locks had grown below his belt in seven years and who rode the red colt as if horse and boy were one.

Rhiannon sat by the horse-mounting block at the Caer of Narberth. Her white garments were stained and tattered, she was bone-skinny and her back swayed from the weight of her task. She was bound by her hair to the bridle ring in the wall. A stableboy brought her water in a bucket and undid the knot of her mane whenever a visitor arrived at the gate.

Tiernon and his wife dismounted. As they drew near, Rhiannon spoke:

"Guests, come no closer. I will carry you into the court, since that is my punishment for killing my son and destroying him with my own hands and consuming him."

24

Tiernon shook his head and stood fast, his hand clutching Gwri's foot in the stirrup. "No, you will not carry us," he said.

Rhiannon let loose her breath and sobbed. She begged Tiernon to tell her why he would not let her carry them, why he would thus increase her trouble.

"Behold your son, Lady," Tiernon answered.

Rhiannon squinted at the child straddling the colt. She saw Pwyll's face and her own full, snow-white hair. Boy and colt shone with an aura like the white winter sun. An aura that revealed them, without a doubt, to be children of the White Night Mare.

A servant ran to fetch the chieftain. Pwyll wept. Once again, the right words left him to speak with his body. He bent low and lifted Rhiannon on his back and carried her into the court.

Then what rejoicing at Caer Narberth!

But the Lord and Lady of Gwent Ys Coed grieved to lose their Gwri White Locks. Pwyll declared that he, and the boy after him, and his sons and their sons, would be forever allied with Tiernon and his people. And after a time, the boy would return to Tiernon to be fostered and trained for manhood.

Pwyll turned to Rhiannon. "What will you name our son?"

The wrens hovered over Rhiannon's white head.

"He will be called Pryderi," she answered. "I name him 'Anxiety.'"

II
Fand

Pryderi ap Pwyll was brought up carefully, and when Pwyll died, Pryderi ruled the seven cantrevs of Dyfed and they were prosperous.

A gannet glides above the cantrevs of Dyfed. Curled away from sea air by some upheaval, it twitches its wings, then banks back toward salt spray.

Rhiannon watches the gannet from her bed of insipid coldness. She is alone, wasted in thought, in the strong grip of years, dragging violently toward the days of grayness. The moonstone round her neck has dulled. Her skin is faded. Her snow-white hair transparent and thin.

The White Night Mare refused to visit her dreams. No longer will she allow the White Lady to visit her nest or mount her. She disdains the crimson apples Rhiannon offers and will not let Rhiannon nuzzle her or stroke her back and forehead and flanks. When Rhiannon tries to catch her, the mare rears and screams and canters away. The White Lady has become human and leaden. It's been too long since she left the Other-world orchard. Abandoned her father Heveydd for love of a mortal chieftain and birthed a mortal child.

Rhiannon thinks of Pwyll's death, weeps at a new angle, then ponders her own end. A strange notion, for death never ventured into the orchard where she was born.

Where there is no autumn and winter,
when Heveydd sat beneath a tree
and a dandruff entered his eye.
Heveydd rubbed.
Drip. Drip.
One tear and then another.
Two saltwater beads fell on his knees.
The third was a pearl.
He caught the iridescent droplet
in his palm and blew on it.
It grew.
It grew to the size of an owl's egg.
He hooted to it.
Owl's song, dog's rough ditty, serpent's tune,
anthem of hart, badger's lyric, hare's vibration,
whale's chanty and madrigal of horse,
until it was padded in infinite music.
Then Heveydd tucked the pearl
into the lair of the White Night Mare and there
Rhiannon incubated, hatched and nested.
Pissed pearls and cried pearls
and the milk she sucked from the Night Mare's teats
was the juice of pearls, too.

In the mortal world,
Rhiannon's pearls
dissolved into water
like that of ordinary women.

Who am I now? Rhiannon wonders. Not an oyster for all my pearls. Neither new velvet nor bumpy spring. Neither am I appetite, aphrodisiac and allure. The alabaster has cracked and puckered. And Pwyll, who loved me even as I aged, is gone.

She lies on her bed, dripping. Tears soak her stretched and sagging body. She squeezes her eyes. Two pearls pop out and flick her chin.

She leaves her bed, dressed all in black. She walks toward the sea cliffs of Dyfed. She leaves her herds. She leaves her son and his young wife. She walks away from the Caer of Narberth, never glancing at the mound, leaving a trail of pearls. And the loyal wrens—who had come with her from the orchard and stayed through the long years and comforted Rhiannon in her anxiety—follow, warbling above her head.

She stands on a cliff and pearls tumble down her cheeks. They ricochet on the rocks, swirl into an eddy on the beach and are drawn by tide into the sea. "No regret," she reminds herself. "I made my choice and lived happy with Pwyll."

But her weeping grows fiercer, until she's howling like an ocean storm. The waves rise to meet her wails and whirl into winds that whip her gown. The black veil slaps her face.

The stream of pearls widens into a river that cuts through the cliff. The glittering white orbs spread over reefs and vault over surf and dance with maelstroms, moving west until they catch first the ear and then the eye of Manannann mac Lir.

The sea god patrols the island of Eriu in his currach, and wherever he imagines the boat to go, so it goes. He makes a mist of his breath to shroud the island from Fomorii invaders.

He hears a mournful song in the distance and wonders if dolphins or selkies have lost a loved one. Then, banging. Like hailstones on drums, beating the hard wicker of his little boat.

Manannann looks down and the currach is trapped in a tangle of pearls. He scoops a handful. He bites one. He glances around and sees no one, but in the east there's a storm. Who but he can create such a squall?

He whistles, and his horses, who can run on foam or on land, rise out of the water, pulling a golden chariot. He jumps into the cart and clicks his tongue. Horses and god streak over the war cries of the strong-haired sea and over the tempest of green waves and over the jaws of the wondrous and bitter ocean to the coast of Dyfed.

Manannann stops short of the beach. He floats on white caps, watching. A woman stands on the cliffs. Weeping pearls. She is the source of this deluge. He rocks with the swells, spying on her through fog, and when the wind snatches the veil from her head, he reaches with his long arm and grabs the black cloth in midair, then swims to shore for a closer look.

Manannann mac Lir gazes at Rhiannon, eyes limp with love and recognition.

"I have never seen a more wonderful woman, so endowed, inside and out," he says, materializing beside her and handing her the sopping veil.

Rhiannon nods in thanks and moves. She savors her solitude. She could not care less who he is, where he came from or what he might want.

"Wait!" the sea god implores. Long ago, Pwyll had called on her to hold still, but she made him cool his heels until he found the right words with which to summon her. No such courtship games will ever interest her again.

His pale skin is blue where Earth's dappled sunlight pinches it. He is long and thin, graceful on sea and in ethers, but not on land. Manannann mac Lir leaps through damp air and dandles in front of her. She turns around and there he is. She turns again. He is there. She cannot escape.

"You are a pearl, even as you weep pearls," he says. "You are the brightest, most beautiful creature in this world or the Other."

"Wipe the seawater from your eyes, lad," she snaps. "And step aside!"

"What?" He is taken aback by her impudence. "I am Manannann, King of the Sea." He glowers at her, full of the pride of rank. But he is softened by love. It has been millennia since he first saw her, glorious upon the White Night Mare, and because he comes from the Land of Promise, he sees her that way still. She is earth and sky. He is sea and sky, and he must have her for his queen. He throws his shoulders back to exhibit his tough, scaly chest.

"Come with me to Tir Tairnigiri." He opens his arms to welcome her, and when she steps back, annoyed, he considers sweeping her into his cloak, the cloak that can catch all the colors in the world.

"I do not answer abrupt questions from boys, even noble and handsome ones like you," she snarls, while the wrens chatter and scold him. She wishes she had her mettlesome mare to carry her off, but her magic is finished.

"No, it's not finished," Manannann says, reading her thoughts. "You've bewitched me, and that is difficult to do, for I am a god of tricks."

"You are a bag of jokes," she says. "Now please, please leave me alone. Let me be. I am old. I'm not flattered." She has work to do. She must discover a future, a way to be aged and alone when her new partner, grief, has finally burned itself out.

"You are not old!" Manannann is shocked at the very idea. "You're like me. You can never be old! How can you, who sucked the White Mare's teat, suck up this human absurdity?"

No more able to resist his impulses than the tide can resist the moon, he pulls at her belt to bring her to him. Rhiannon balks. If he does not leave soon, she'll explode. He has raised her temper from the place where it was buried long ago, where it rested unkindled in the serenity of her years with Pwyll, after their son returned.

And this surprising reappearance of her mare's fire begins to interest her.

"I am about to be a grandmother," she announces grandly.

"Oh, well," he replies. "I am grandfather, great-grandfather and great-great-grandfather to many. Come to Tir Tairnigiri and see."

"Have you no pity?" Rhiannon replies, and the pearls bubble up in her eyes again. "Go back where you came from."

He smiles and stands his ground, although, in his white-bronze, webbed sea shoes, he teeters a bit. Rhiannon, whose own feet are hard as hooves and solidly laid, suppresses the urge to laugh.

"I am decrepit and exhausted at having to remind you of that fact. I am human, Manannann. I gave up immortality and youth for Pwyll. Soon I will die."

"You are wrong! You will never die. Your age is delusion. Time hangs in the mortal world like dark clouds about to rain. But in *our* world, time curls like a serpent biting its tail. You can't unbind your origins. Surrender, Rhiannon!" And with that enthusiasm, he wobbles wildly and nearly topples.

"What are these pearls, if not proof of your Otherworldliness?" he asks, regaining his balance.

"They are a fluke and an evil reminder of my pain, probably sent by my angry father."

"Nonsense! Pwyll has died and you are released to return to us. Come with me and you'll see that the youth you think you've lost is not gone." He leans closer. "With me you'll be happier than you have ever been. Forever."

Rhiannon sighs. She has only to look in a glass to know that the choice she made is final. "This is cruel teasing," she says, "and you are a heartless, upstart child, O mighty King of the Sea."

She sits on a rock and cups her head in her hands. Pearls sprint from her eyes. "Go away," she blubbers. "Go away."

Instead of going away, he blathers on and on, pacing like a penguin, waving his reedy arms, sketching pictures on the clouds to illustrate his home: gleaming turrets and towers of high-polished shell, flocks of lapis angelfish shepherded by mermaids, mermen warriors with sharks for steeds, ivory unicorn whales, unfathomably graceful orange coral reefs, undulating forests of turquoise algae, the richness and underwater magnificence of his kingdom.

She is reminded of the orchard in the Otherworld under the mound and unsure whether his pictures of that Otherworld perfection make her nostalgic or claustrophobic. Her stomach twists when he offers his home to her and more. She is quiet. She has decided to be patient as a clod of earth, hoping he'll wear himself out.

He cups water in his palm to make a mirror. Here is her face, young as apple blossoms. "You see," he says, "you never changed." She smashes his hands with her fist and the water shatters. He reaches for her.

"How dare you take such liberties with an old and widowed woman?" she shrieks. "How dare you behave like this to the Queen of Dyfed!"

"No longer, for your son is king and he has a new queen."

"Yes," she sighs. "I am displaced."

He laughs. "Not in Tir Tairnigiri! If I can give you now a gift of your own choosing, will you at least come with me to see my land and sleep with me one night?"

"What I want, you cannot do," she says, trying to think quickly of a task that might finally get rid of him.

"I can do anything," Manannann brags.

"Then build me a circle of high, broad standing stones in honor of my husband, Pwyll. And within the circle, embed a sheaf of wheat in a lodestone, that my son's land will thrive, always abundant. Then I will go with you."

"Done!" he shouts. And from his waist he pulls a bag made of crane skin. He empties it and outlines a circle of silver net, starfish and spirit catchers made of clams. He roars like a breaker smashing against rock and shakes his cloak.

"There! You have your wish, Rhiannon. Come, let us go now!"

The monument to Pwyll is more eloquent than Rhiannon could ever have envisaged. She blinks at Manannann, who grins proudly. She weeps again. She makes a pail of her skirt to catch the pearls, to offer them to her husband's memory.

She shuffles slowly toward the circle, pearls clattering in her gown. The wrens hop from one upright stone to the next, then dive toward the wheat sheaf and pluck it up, and suddenly, the structure shudders and wavers, melts and turns to pond.

"You liar!" Rhiannon spins to face the sea god. "You would not know water from wood or a goat from a flounder, or corn from a kipper, or a peach from a prawn! You created an hallucination to fool me into going with you. Get out! You have no hold on me!"

"There is nothing I can't do," Manannann sniffs. "Let me try again. If it hadn't been for those birds of yours . . ." And he takes a little bow and arrow from his crane-skin bag and points them at Rhiannon's wrens.

"You can't kill them," Rhiannon says calmly, but she is not at all certain whether they may have become as mortal as she. Yet how have they hung about these many years?

"All right. I give you leave to try again," Rhiannon says, truly curious now as to what and who she has become, what and who she might still be and why, indeed, her fluids are once again pearls.

"Build the stone circle as strong and real as Pwyll, do it right this time, and I will go with you to Tir Tairnigiri."

"Do you swear?" Manannann asks.

"I do," she replies, "but I'm safe, for I'm sure that you, with your ocean conjuring and sea chicanery, cannot ever make a solid thing."

Rhiannon collapses on her rock and wraps the black veil, starched with salt, tight around her head. She stares listlessly at the horizon, mapping the flight of the gannet. She dreams of Pwyll. She wishes death would take her, too. Take her to him.

To his surprise, Manannann is uncertain whether he can satisfy the request of this female caught between mortality and eternity. He whose moods mimic sea changes—who has seduced many a human woman and sired many a half-human child (and saved many a human warrior with his marvelous sword, the Answerer)—has never been so determined, desirous or insecure. He is enamored and glamoured by Rhiannon. He would perform any task in exchange for the White Lady's caresses, to win her affectionate murmurs. If it is standing stones she wants, he will find them and bring them and make a monument to that precious dead husband of hers.

There is nothing he won't do, Manannann announces to himself. But how will he do this?

The sea king is drying out. Desiccating. He is itchy and thirsty under the Earth sky. He cannot tolerate land for long. He rushes to the ocean and flops into the water. Relief. He calls his currach, climbs in and sits, bobbing and thinking, chin on knees. She has dissolved his illusion and would surely uncover another trick. Even if he could work true stone—which he cannot, because rock is alien and too heavy for his sea body or any sea magic—there are no stones in Dyfed large enough for the megalith Rhiannon requires.

Hours pass. Rhiannon languishes, staring at the sky, ignoring him, confident that he will fail. Failure is unbearable to him. A sea mew lands on Manannann's head and scratches it for him. He thinks and thinks and his thoughts call up four nymphs who croon:

Come with us, Manannann mac Lir, and you will obtain your mind's design.

He spreads his cloak into wings and lifts off the little boat. Skimming billows, inhaling spume, he follows the nymphs until they come to Eriu, where they dip through Manannann's protective shroud of mist. The nymphs lead the sea king across meadows, along winding rivers and sparkling fields of cowslip to another shore, then over another chilly sea to the island of Tory, to the foot of a mountain.

And in the shafts of that mountain, sixty Fomorii snore upon sixty stone slabs.

Manannann is dizzy and flaking. If ever there was a trial, this is it. He has gone farther inland than he has ever been. The nymphs disappear and Manannann roosts on a rock, splashing himself with dew, thinking, thinking, devising a way to get the Fomorii and their stones back to Dyfed. No Fomor will travel unless there's some enticement: delectable De Danann blood or the shiny slather of jewels. Manannann thinks and thinks, wrapped round with his cloak, thinking until his brain conjures three geese, who nip at his ankles and rasp:

Come with us, Manannann mac Lir, and you will obtain your mind's design.

Manannann waddles slowly behind the geese, tottering in his white-bronze, webbed sea shoes. Now they fly; now they tramp across grasses and fragrant heather, slipping up hillock, down dale, to the end of the rainbow, where the geese leave him beside a cavern that plunges away, away, below the sea, in the hot bowels of the Earth. Manannann is horrified. He has visited the hollows of the Daghda, but he has never been this deep in dirt. He coughs and chokes and fights for air. His fish flesh sweats. His throat clenches around the stench of sulfur.

In the cave, in the smoky dark, with stinging eyes, Manannann passes chamber after chamber, each containing a thousand golden pots brimming with jewels. He stumbles on, terrified, until his fear of tunnels gives birth at last to two blind moles, glowing like candles, who troll with their tiny teeth at his cloak and squeak:

Come with us, Manannann mac Lir, and you will obtain your mind's design.

Trembling and tripping, Manannann, brave King of the Sea, follows the moles through gruesome galleries and caliginous corridors until they come to the Hall of Priceless Illusion, where Manannann seizes a handful of treasure and comes up empty-handed.

And this is truly a wonder, for even the master of deception has been duped. He unknots the crane-skin bag on his belt. He reaches into it, and pulls out an illusion, then piles illusion upon illusion, until he has a portable mirage.

Back again he toils, through tunnels and out of the mountain, goose-stepping back across the grasses and meadows, flying along rivers and across estuaries, back to the foot of the mountain of the Fomorii, where Manannann hangs a pot of jewels on the precipice above their door.

When they awaken, the one-eyed behemoths drool and scutter and fall over and under and into one another, reaching for the unreachable riches, forgoing their breakfasts of fresh faerie babes, just for a taste of this wealth.

From his perch in a tree, Manannann calls to the brutes and

offers them the jewels, if only they'll bring their stone beds and follow him.

He carries the fanciful gems, down hillock, up dale and across fragrant fields, while the sixty Fomorii stamp on their single legs behind him, stone slabs strapped to their hairy chests.

They reach the chilly sea, where, with a wheeze of gratitude, Manannann swims into his element, and the Fomorii follow, rowing their rocks with their arms across the waves to the shore where Rhiannon sits and broods.

Manannann soars above the giants' heads, dangling the Priceless Illusion like turnips before mules, the prize for placing one dolmen upon two, posts and lintels balanced into arches conjunct with constellations. And within the outer circle, they place a smaller one, and within that, a third round, until all the stones are upright and secured.

Then he shakes the Priceless Illusion before the sixty behemoths and leads them back to the sea. He leads them along awhile from his currach to a sound where the water yawns deeper than the hugest Fomor is high. They paddle and kick their single legs, scudding and spattering after the fast-evaporating treasure, but without their slab barges, the Fomorii drown halfway home to Tory.

Manannann returns to his palace. He dresses in his invulnerable armor with his invincible sword, the Answerer. He carries his helmet under one arm, and with the other he drags a lodestone from the sea floor and hauls it all the long, panting way to the center of the stone circle. Laboring mightily, without the magic of his crane-skin bag, he presses the Answerer flat into the lodestone to make an indentation. He places a wheat sheaf in the cavity shaped like his sword. He pours salt from his helmet onto the wheat and thaws it with hot breath, then cools it with cold breath, until it dries to a crystal sheen.

He floats to Rhiannon and stands in front of her. "My lady," he says softly. She looks up, pleased that he is at least respectful.

"See there," he says, pointing. "Your circle. Go test it. Set your birds on it. It is solid. Rock that will never crumble, and within it, encased in thick glass, is the wheat sheaf for abundance."

Rhiannon rises. Cautious, not to be fooled again. But she fills her black veil with blue pebbles from the beach and pearls from her eyes. She rubs against each stone, like a horse against a scratching post. The birds fly round and round. They peck at the sheaf. They cannot move it. Rhiannon strolls through the circles, spreading white pearls and blue pebbles in a spiral. Pearls and pebbles hum, infinite music that blends earth and sky, sea and sky. She chants poems to Pwyll and blessings upon the Earth. She scratches an ogham into the lodestone.

Manannann watches with unfamiliar patience until her grief and brief mortal happiness are etched into the monument. The wrens perch on her shoulders and she speaks to them in whispers. She leaves them in the circle to wait for her and guard it.

Then Rhiannon walks to Manannann,
stripping her mourning garments as she goes.
She takes his hand and walks with him into the sea.
Waist-high in water, she wraps her legs
around Manannann mac Lir.
The sea god enters her murky chasm.
Thus attached, they are propelled farther and farther
into the ocean that hollowed the land
where she once dwelled.

They sink down and down.
He plants his salty seed in her.
Her skin shimmers like pearls.
Mortal age washes from her filmy face.
Empress of Tides,
The White Lady of the White Night Mare
mounts a sea horse
and rides with Manannann mac Lir
into Tir Tairnigiri,
the shadowy Land of Promise,
somewhere between the shores of Dyfed and Eriu.

And there she's called Fand, Pearl of Beauty.

III
Emer

Fand lived with Manannann mac Lir under the sea and was content for a time. But Manannann's moods switched like a cod's tail and he left her for another. Fand went to a drifting island, where she lived alone with her wrens.

I've lost my voice. The Drink of Oblivion the druids gave us obscures my story, but not my pain. CuChulainn drank it to forget Fand. I drank it to forget he loved her. Thus, I have no words to remind my husband of my jealousy. Forgiveness will come because it must. But I will not truly forget.

I won't forget the day he came to court me. Emer. Daughter of Forgall the Wily, and considered a Tara among women. I was brought up in the ancient virtues, in stateliness and grace. I was carefully tutored in the seven gifts of womanhood: beauty, strength, sweet speech, cleverness, wisdom, modesty and fidelity. I wish those contrivances could shore my heart against sorrow and resentment.

Now CuChulainn lies wasting in sickness on his bedbox. I

watch over him. I put cold compresses to his head. I wash his arms and legs in cool water that can only remind me of Fand of the Sea. CuChulainn tosses and groans and sweats on the mattress I made for him, ticked with the softest grasses I picked with my own hand. In his delirium, he battles puffballs and phantoms. Has the potion merely dampened his will? Is he still mad for love of Fand?

It was a pretty afternoon, streaked with easy sunlight that framed a pretty picture of maidens bevied in the courtyard of Forgall's fortress. We gathered as young girls do, laughing, playing, comparing our stitches. Some sewed embroideries. Others laid down their needlework to gossip. Some played ball. Others picked flowers to braid into one another's hair.

Thunder. The ground shook. Maids shivered and shrieked running in from the coming rain. But my sister insisted the pounding noise was horses' hooves and climbed the rampart to look.

"Emer! Emer! A chariot!" she cried. "Drawn by two steeds, one gray and one black. And two persons in it. Look!" She pointed at the road below. "I can see them clearly now. One is dark and sad, clad in a scarlet cloak with a brooch of gold. He's got a blazing scarlet shield with a silver rim wrought with figures of beasts. It is magnificent! His charioteer is tall and slender with curling red hair held by a fillet of bronze. He has gold plates on either side of his face. Oh, Emer! He urges the horses with a goad of pure gold!"

"That one must be Laeg," another said. "And the dark warrior is called the Hound of Ulster."

The girls twittered and giggled and composed their faces. Every woman, married or maiden, old or young, was bewitched by CuChulainn. I knew he had come for me.

I rose to meet him as they strode in the gates.

"May the path be smooth before you," I said.

"And you," CuChulainn replied, "may you be safe from harm." The briefest of greetings as my bright eye met his melancholy one. He glanced at my bodice and stretched his hand toward it. He was forthcoming in his purpose; he has never denied his desires. Though we spoke in riddles, we both knew the reason for this abrupt visit. We both knew the outcome.

"Fair is the plain," he said, placing a gentle finger between my breasts. "I would rest my sword here."

"No one comes to this plain," I answered, "who has not slain his hundreds."

"This is a sweet territory," he said, "where I would lay my head."

"No one visits this territory," I replied, "who has not proven himself in mighty deeds, and your deeds are still to come."

Back and forth we went, making our plans with friendly argument and boasting, exchanging demands, scheming in riddles. Forgall would never let me marry CuChulainn. He would have to carry me forcibly from Forgall's fortress.

I loved him the minute I saw him. But not for me and my life was some untried lad, ornamented though he was in grand style. He must earn higher status, become more than an extraordinary boy, prove his hero's worth. All this I informed him in so many words.

"Whatever you want, I will do," CuChulainn promised.

"Then I'll accept your offer."

"He is too young, too strong, too beautiful! The answer is *no*!" Forgall declared when he heard of CuChulainn's visit. "His only property is vanity. He brags that he was fostered by heroes and kings. Some say his father is Lugh Sungod himself. But he's merely a bastard boy, ill-bred and headstrong. He will not have Emer!"

I smiled secretly to myself.

Besides—Forgall ranted on—my older sister was still unmarried and I was not to go first, that is improper. Then my father set out to trick CuChulainn and send him into death.

All things are ordained. Our love riddles had set our destiny. My father's trick turned back on him.

Forgall arranged to send CuChulainn for training on Skye, with Scatach the Shadow Woman. She does not take kindly to strangers. My father sent my brothers, with false friendship, to accompany CuChulainn. They deserted him to hang on Scatach's swift, barbed pike.

But the Hound of Ulster outwitted them all. He crossed the Bridge of Leaps, as none had done before, and entered the fortress of the Shadowy One. She was impressed. She agreed to teach him the fine arts of war. She taught him to use the *gae bolg*, the belly spear, then gave him the dreadful weapon. He fought her opponents. One of them was Aifa, whom even Scatach feared. Their single combat, wrestling and rolling in each other's arms, ended as a love match and peace was made, a son conceived. That was the first infidelity, though we were yet only promised in riddles.

He had proved himself a hero beyond measure. He returned to apply his skills to fetch me from my father's home.

I won't forget how he leaped the hero's salmon leap over the high ramparts of Forgall's dun and dealt three blows. Each blow slaughtered eight men. I dashed through the clash of spears and swords, hitching my skirts to jump over bodies and into CuChulainn's chariot. Laeg leered at me and whipped the black and gray horses, faster and faster toward Emain Macha.

Forgall sent his hosts to follow us. CuChulainn's battle fury came hard on him. Berserk and raging, he massacred so many, the ford ran red and Forgall retreated.

CuChulainn is the bravest of Ulster's warriors. But there is another kind of courage he lacks.

He won me as I'd wished to be won. I was free and clear of my father. We wove our bones and fortunes around and through one another like wicker. We had no rivals; none could best the delight we had in each other. We were the envy of every household. "He, so handsome and heroic. She, so beautiful and gifted." And the king laid property, rank and wealth on CuChulainn.

CuChulainn leaned against a pillar stone, polishing his shield, concentrating on each silver beast, when three messengers arrived. Three golden wrens who spoke aloud.

"We are sent by Fand, Queen of the Sea, wife of Manannann mac Lir, who is alone on her island and beset by enemies. She begs you to come, to fight for one day on her behalf."

What did I know of Fand? What did I care, except for the creeping fear that one battle, one day, would be CuChulainn's last.

CuChulainn refused. "She is Manannann's wife, let him

protect her," he told the wrens, who fluttered and squawked in protest. "I have my own wife to protect," he said. From his leaning post, he stretched his toe to my leg and tickled my thigh. I laughed, but the wrens set up such a cry that, at last, CuChulainn sought Laeg and sent him to spy out the land and Fand's situation. The wrens guided the charioteer to the drifting island and that, I thought, was the end of that.

Oh, but for her persistence and the seduction of the Other-world, a maelstrom of splendor that bleeds away all things real and ordinary!

When Laeg returned, he told CuChulainn: "If every inch of Ireland were mine, if I had supreme rule over its fair inhabitants, I would give it up without regret to live with Fand. I would, without hesitation, rid her of her enemies and do anything else she wanted, for her husband has deserted her and she, the fairest woman in this world or the Other, is helpless." And Laeg went on and on into the night describing the wonders of Fand. With every drop of mead, she grew more glorious.

I forgive CuChulainn because I must, because forgiveness is at the core of love, and life between us cannot go on without it. I will never forgive Laeg.

My father spoke true when he said CuChulainn's richest property is vanity. And it is impossible to discourage the Hound of Ulster from adventuring. Neither would I have wanted to. He is curious and impetuous. Those qualities in him that I love best are the same that sunder my heart.

Fight for a day, indeed! CuChulainn was gone from one full moon to the next. I pined. I dreamed of the Otherworld. I saw them together in her radiant glass bed with stars dancing on the blankets. I denied it. I went about my daily duties, merry and singing with the maidens who attended me, modest and sweet of speech. So much time passed, I thought perhaps this adventure had been his last, for it is prophesied that CuChulainn will not live long, but that his young death will presage eternal fame. Day after day I watched the road and the sea, and still my Hound of Ulster did not return to bay of his exploits and lick my hands and breasts.

Sorrow on sorrow, depression is on me. Downcast for my handsome young man, the dark, scarlet-cloaked warrior, who loved me above the others and was charmed away by the music of birds.

I thought the rider who dragged into Emain Macha must be a messenger come to tell me of CuChulainn's death. But it was the Hound himself, reluctant, different. His look was not of one who is battle-worn, nor was it the look of one who has outgrown his youth. It was the spell of love. I embraced him, ecstatic to see him, but his touch was cool and distracted. I kissed him and he returned my kiss with open eyes staring far over my shoulder. I pattered and chatted at him, pretending nothing had changed. I poured his drink and brought him meat, but the sadness that had fled when we were married had returned. He grieved, inconsolable, and would not tell me why.

My heart also grew grave. I knew, though I could not admit

or ask him, that he was yearning for love of Fand, and that in his month's absence, he had not only fought her enemies but created mine. And who were her enemies? Loneliness, solitude and a mercurial husband.

In winter, near Samhain, my sister and I sat sewing by the hearth while CuChulainn and Laeg stood out-of-doors, talking in deep whispers. My sister! Ever a lookout, wily as our father. She crept to the door. She saw three wrens above CuChulainn's head. She opened the door a wee crack and pressed her ear against it. She heard the birds arrange a tryst by the yew tree at the head of Baile's Strand. She hopped back to her place beside me, just as CuChulainn stomped in the door, shaking the chill rain from his dark hair. Without a word, he reached for his scarlet cloak and left. I opened my mouth to stop him, to ask where he was going, but my sister quieted me. The clangor of the departing chariot drowned my sobs.

I gathered forty-nine maidens. I whetted fifty knives until they glowered. I chose the largest, sharpest weapon for myself. We fifty marched to Baile's Strand.

An icy moon shone above CuChulainn and Fand. Winter stars sparkled around her, and she, shimmering as if carved from pearl, held his hands, all in a dream. Her wrens flitted in and out of the white light that emanated from her, warbling coy songs of love.

And I, a nightmare fury, rampaged across the strand. Screaming curses and taunts, naked, heated by rage, wielding our knives and torches, we fifty surrounded Fand, while CuChulainn leaped to protect her. I won't forget how he had once refused her, because she had her own husband to protect her.

With one vault and swirl, he scattered my forty-nine women. Then, weakened by the sight of me and by my jeering wrath, he stepped aside, not meaning to, so I stepped into his place. I put my knife to Fand's ivory throat. It was CuChulainn who should have been my target.

Once I had been sure of my beauty, but now that I was face-to-face with the Queen of the Sea, who had robbed me of my man, all my conceits and confidence dropped like a stone from my belly, and my face seemed to twist into monstrous, clumsy ugliness.

"What has led you, Hound of Ulster," I hissed between gritted teeth, "to shame me before the women of Eriu and all honorable people? I came under your shelter, trusting in your faithfulness, believing in your love, and now you rush to her. You are no hound but an unweaned pup!"

CuChulainn stammered and protested. My hero is too young, too strong, too beautiful. Why, he stuttered, would I not be content to take my turn with other women? And this one could only flatter me, make me look better, for she is incomparably lovely and moreover a queen of the Otherworld.

Fand stood quietly, head high, like a mare proud and patient who pities the one who rides her. But white tears brimmed in her eyes. I pressed my knife a little deeper into her throat, and the metal seemed to convey a sympathy between our hearts. Sorrow on sorrow. What was hers? Was she remembering the mortal husband who had died? Or the immortal who had left her for another? Were her footsteps, like mine, laced with anger when she paced alone through the halls of her house, torn and wretched for lack of love?

I loosened my grip on the dagger and faced CuChulainn. "If you want this woman, take her! I know that everything new is dazzling and everything common seems bitter. What we do not have, we want, and what we possess, we belittle. You have shamed and demeaned me!"

A mist passed overhead. At first it looked like a bird, and then like a shapeless mass of light.

CuChulainn blinked as if I'd presented a riddle he could guess. "But Emer, you are still pleasing to me and will be as long as I live," he said. His words lifted like a question. Had I not understood that nothing had changed and that this love of his for Fand merely meant more, not less?

"CuChulainn!" I shouted. "Are you deaf? Are your ears stuffed with salt water? Hear me! I may not be the wife of a sea god, or live in the fanciful Land of Promise. Nor will I be young forever. I do not glitter and gleam like an ocean mirage. But I was raised in rank to be a queen and I would rather be dead than abandoned, rather be abandoned than second best!"

The passing mist grew darker and assumed the shape of a trumpet.

"Leave me, then, CuChulainn," Fand said. We gasped, surprised by the strange, despairing gurgle in her voice. "It is I who shall be abandoned. Heaven touches Earth by means of rain. It is terrible to love and not be cherished in return. You, Emer, are truly CuChulainn's wife. I will go, though I would rather stay with CuChulainn than live in the sunny home of the gods. Emer, he is yours."

"No, *yours*. And you are welcome to him—" I began, but Laeg piped up and shook his finger at me.

"It was not well of you, Emer, to come to kill Fand in her misery."

"Then I will kill you, instead. I'll scrape off your freckles, one by one, and rip each of your curly locks from your scalp!" I lashed toward Laeg in a fresh rage.

It was a sudden burst of wind and sea which knocked Laeg to the ground and saved his contemptible life. The Horseman of the Crested Wave appeared in the frosty air above us. We gaped at him, for he was tall as cliffs and glowing. His long green hair swept about him, as light as his feet when he landed before Fand.

"What's this?" he said. "Is CuChulainn the slitter in a game of hurling?"

He laughed and a host of little clouds, like fantastic seabirds, puffins and auklets, bobbed in the sky. Then Manannann mac Lir asked his wife's pardon. I won't forget that CuChulainn has never asked mine. The King of the Sea, humble as plankton, begged Fand to remember their happiness and swore he'd never leave her, never again subject her to his breezy whims. In her eyes, amusement, for she knew he spoke true . . . until the weather broke.

He hovered, competing for space with Fand's wrens. He shooed them away. "Will you return to me and Tir Tairnigiri?" he asked.

The White Lady sighed. "Love is a vain thing and vanishes quickly," she said. "You are dear to me, Manannann. You are completely mine *when* you are mine, and that is probably the most I can hope for. Looking at the two of you, I think neither man is better or nobler than the other. I'll go with you, Manannann, for you have no stable mate, but CuChulainn has Emer."

Wind picked up. The sky was blown into ribbons of pallor, edged with nameless, weightless no-hue's-land. Manannann beamed, triumphant, and kissed his Pearl of Beauty. The Hound of Ulster slumped, a dry, discarded lump about to crumble, his hero's antics useless here. Manannann shook his cloak between Fand and CuChulainn—the cloak that can catch all the colors in the world—so that they would never meet again or recognize each other if they did. Then he scooped Fand under one arm. So small she seemed a tiny sea horse in his embrace. She folded her pale arms around his neck, smiling ever so slightly, and nuzzled her chin in his beard. And they were gone.

Harsher words than Fand's have never been spoken, for CuChulainn was disconsolate and no more loving of me than he'd been after his visit to the drifting island. I wonder: Had cleverness failed me against the seventh gift of womanhood—fidelity? Might I not have taken a lesson from Fand and found a new lover, too? A hero fine as CuChulainn. Perhaps Manannann mac Lir himself!

Ah, but wiliness was not given to me.

CuChulainn wandered, sorrow on sorrow, through the mountains of Munster, in the hills of death, neither eating nor drinking until Laeg found him and returned him to me.

The druids gave us the Drink of Oblivion and immediately upon swallowing it, CuChulainn fell into this wasting sickness. He writhes as if he were whipped by horses' goads. He moans and flails. Time rebukes us for our faults. Time stitches the torn fabric that binds us. I watch over him but cannot forget.

Do I want him? Do I want half a heart? At least he won't live long.

"The Wren's Triad" retold from versions of *The Mabinogion*, the *Táin Bó Cuailnge*, *The Yellow Book of Lecan* and *The White Goddess*. From Brian Merriman, Padraic Colum, Charles Squire and Mairi Nighean Alasdair Ruaidh (translated by John Wright).

CERRIDWEN

S peak of your own mother as you like. Describe her however you please. Call her a bitch, a cow, a cat, a rat, vermin of any kind, a vixen, a crow or a nanny goat.

My mother was a sow.

I am a word in a book; the light in a lantern; the string of a harp; Taliesin. . . .

A pig who possessed the holy cauldron of inspiration. Life-in-death and death-in-life. So old she never aged. So ferocious, she killed me to birth me.

Whose is the birth that has never been discharged and never will? . . .

She was Cerridwen. Mother of Nine Waves. Mother of the Spring. Mother of the Willow. Mother of Creirwyn, the most beautiful girl in the world. Mother of Afgaddu, the ugliest boy on Earth.

I am a thorn beneath the nail; a flood across a plain. . . .

Afgaddu, named for the Black Raven. No beauty of beasts had he. The raven is a sleek, glorious, stately creature. Not Afgaddu.

I am a boar, ruthless and red; a breaker, threatening doom. . . .

Even his mother could not bear to lay eyes on him for long. She who brought the sunshine and blossoms, the thunder and ice. If her son was to be hideous, she would find him other gifts—Cerridwen would obtain the Muse for Afgaddu. She would make him unforgettable, irresistible, for he would be chief of bards, a prophet, decider of the fates of kings.

I am a salmon in a pool; a hill where poets walk. . . .

Cerridwen rocked her ugly baby. She sang to him. And in her lullabies, she promised him a divine future.

I am an infant: who but I peeps from the unhewn dolmen arch? . . .

Each night after Afgaddu fell asleep, Cerridwen wrapped herself in her finest linen mantle and crept outside to commune with her sacred companions, the pigs. There, under the whistling trees, surrounded by the encouraging magic of other sows, cheered on by their mystical snorts and grunts, she raised her arms and chanted:

I have been in many shapes before I attained this form
Without flesh, without bone
Without vein, without blood
Without head, without feet

Wide as the surface of the Earth
In shelter linger
privet and pine
I am the hoofed beast at this enchanted time!

The last words spun from her mouth. Cerridwen dropped to the ground. Her feet and hands cleaved and hardened and she was transformed from a large, ungainly woman—the descendant of giants—into a marvelous white sow with crescent tusks to mirror the moon, hairy snout and low-slung gallop.

She roamed the musty, spidery woods, seeking the mound where the formula of knowledge and inspiration was hidden among the mushrooms and fallen leaves; she truffled in the moist, rich loam and over the grassy fields, night after night.

Until one night, in the eerie dark of the moon, she tripped on a stone. She kicked her hooves to clear the leaves. The stone was no mute rock but a carved tablet.

I am a stag of seven tines; a tear the sun lets fall. . . .

She had searched for months. Now, at last, Cerridwen found the spell she sought. She stood on her hinds legs, she snuffled and sneezed, she changed back into a woman and dragged the tablet home.

I am firmament, element, language; the spirit of skillful
gift. . . .

While her household was still asleep and snoring, Cerridwen

traced the tablet's etchings by firelight until she solved their puzzle.

Day after day, she wandered the forests, orchards and hills, the shore and meadows, guided by the ogham scratched upon the stone and by the stars and planets. She gathered herbs and insects and salamanders, moss from the cornerstones of ancient caers, mistletoe, bark of oak and rowan and yew, the feces of horses, fungus, the velvet of deer's antlers.

She laid the ingredients in that cauldron which had come to her from giants. She set the mixture to simmer for a year and a day. I was the boy she brought from the village to stir the pot while she hunted for fresh roots and berries, flowers and leaves of every season.

I am a hawk falling above a cliff; I know the names of the stars from north curved out and into south. . . .

I was, and will always be, in some part of me, Gwion, the neighbor's dull son. Certainly, Cerridwen would murder me when the brew was done. But I was an innocent boy, the child of innocent folk, who knew nothing of cauldrons or sow's appetites, so I stirred on and on for meager pay, day after day.

Until one day, at the end of the year, three burning drops spat out of the cauldron and stung my thumb.

I am a spear that roars for blood; I was loquacious before I could speak. . . .

At once, of course, I thrust my finger into my mouth. And at once, I understood the nature and meaning of all things past, present and future. I also realized that Cerridwen would soon know that I, Gwion the Pot-stirrer, now had the gifts that were meant for Afgaddu.

I am a blaze on every hill; I have been in stocks and fetters for a year and a day. . . .

Whatever beastly name you call your mother, whoever she is, you know it is the first rule of life that you never, ever, come between mother and child. Even the pig, who feeds on her litter, protects it with her life. Her offspring are hers alone to consume.

I am the shield for every head; I instruct half the universe. . . .

I left the spitting, boiling cauldron and ran into the forest. As soon as she looked into it, Cerridwen saw what had happened and dashed out of the house, a screaming blue hag shrieking "Gwion! Gwion!" hair afire and red blotches on her cheeks, her fingers tapered as knives.

I am a tide that drags to death; I am winged by genius. . . .

With Cerridwen hot on my heels, I wished hard to be a creature nimble and quick, and suddenly, I shrank. Soft brown hair sprouted over my whole flesh, my ears sprang up. A puffed tail and a wet nose. A rabbit; I bounded along the ground.

I felt a hot breath. I glanced behind me.

Cerridwen was a greyhound, inches from my throat, dog teeth bared, snarling, drooling.

I dived into a river and the current swept me up.

Now, naturally, I wished I were a fish. Lo and behold, my

body lengthened. Scales and fins appeared where there had been fur and feet. I curved and curled along the rush of water. I looked behind me and Cerridwen was an otter. Grinning, swirling, teasing, swimming on her back, not inches from my tail.

With all the wit in the world acquired from those three drops, I still had not learned to use my brains. I was a child, only newly struck by brilliance, but I had imagination enough to wish myself into a bird. One by one, my scales turned to quills. I rose out of the water and flew into the air as a sparrow.

Cerridwen never stopped, but exchanged her fur for the feathers and the talons of a hawk and pursued me.

I pumped my wings. I squeaked with terror as Cerridwen swooped closer and closer. I sighed and dropped from the sky like a pebble and fell to Earth in a barnyard, wishing myself into a grain of wheat, anonymous among all the scattered kerns.

Foolish boy.

Cerridwen, Lady of Grain, chuckled and floated on the air in luxurious circles, taking her time, gliding slowly, lower and lower until her claws skimmed the ground and her sleek raptor body fattened into that of a plump hen, who pecked along the barnyard, and pecked and pecked. And ate me.

I am the womb of every holt; I am the queen of every hive. . . .

Then she returned to her human shape and went home.

Before other mishaps could occur, she gave the remaining potion to Afgaddu. But I, with my tiny, splattered thumbnail, had gotten the lion's share of knowledge and inspiration.

Afgaddu grew up to be a swineherd, and therefore an oracle and a fine magician. Still ugly.

I am a wizard: who but I sets the cool head aflame with smoke? . . .

Nine months later to the day she had eaten me, Cerridwen gave birth to another baby boy. She could not bear to kill me, for I was the most beautiful boy in the world. She tied me in a handbag made of crane skin and dropped me into the sea to my destiny.

I am a lure from Paradise; it is not known if my body is flesh or fish. . . .

I was carried along the tide to the far shore of the bay, where a fisherman, a chieftain named Elphin, netted me. He had caught no fish that day, but one look at the infant in the bag and he felt well rewarded. He named me Taliesin, Radiant Brow.

I shall be upon the Earth until the Day of Doom; and then? . . .

I am chief of bards, a prophet, decider of the fates of kings. I harvest the past. I foretell the future when the land will be laid to waste; the wilderness empty, desolate, the fruit groves barren, the rivers dry, the meadows turned to dust, the forests withered, the mountains crumbled, the Earth and mothers dishonored, the pig disgraced.

Who but I am the weaving god who mends the seam of wounds?

Retold with thanks to Norene Berry and Nancy Robertson.

BLODEUWEDD

The name Llew means "bright," "shining"; Blodeuwedd means "flowers," and Blodeu "bower"; *morwyn* means "little girl."

PREFACE

Long, long ago in Wales, there lived a goddess named Aran-rhod, who insisted on her virginity.

Math the Magician, ruler of all the land, required virgins as footstools to ease his impotence. Shrubbery, nests of baby mice or a mushroom might have worked just as well, but it was virgins Math demanded. Having lost his last maiden to a love affair, he now sought a fresh prie-dieu of unquestionable purity. To prove it, he put prospective employees to a wand-leaping test, wherein Math's divining rod wriggled on the floor like a snake if the morwyn *had known a man.*

"It's hard to find good help these days," Math lamented as girl after girl failed the exam. Although previously no one had much cared about this virgo intacta *business, unfortunately, Math's personal problems were beginning to affect social mores, causing folk to wonder if there wasn't something to this notion of virtue, after all. Maybe young women ought to be looking after their hymens and their so-called honor. This was a limnal era in the history of gods and goddesses; things were changing right and left.*

At any rate, Math's acolyte and nephew Gwydyon offered his sister Aranrhod, an avowed virgin. She came to Math's court, resentful but confident.

As Aranrhod leaped over the stick, a baby boy dropped from beneath her skirts. Math grabbed for it, but it ran away into the sea. This child became the god Dylan. His fate is another tale for another time.

No one saw Gwydyon snatch up a second, smaller infant that slipped from Aranrhod as she stalked from Math's hall. Gwydyon tucked the baby into his cloak, sneaked away from the ruckus and hid it in a closet in his chamber. It was so small, no bigger than a walnut, that he forgot all about it, until one night he heard it cry, then saw a tiny fist poke out from under rumpled clothing. Immediately, Gwydyon wanted the child. Here was a son in whom he could vest all his knowledge and desires, his hopes for the future.

"Get out of my house with that creature!" Aranrhod shouted at Gwydyon, who held the beautiful baby up for approval. "I'm not interested in children. I don't care to be saddled with nappies and nursing!" She stamped her foot and turned her back. "What's more, it's a boy! What do I want with a boy when I have sworn to live only with women?"

Aranrhod pointed toward the door and glowered at her brother.

"Leave now and take that squalling mess with you!"

"The child will be outcast," Gwydyon protested. "He won't exist without a name bestowed on him by his mother. That's the law."

"Let him be nameless."

"You are an evil, wicked, unnatural mother."

"Piffle! I am not a mother at all! I'm a virgin. Whether I've had relations with a man has nothing to do with it and is nobody's business but my own. You've been around Uncle Math too long. I am a virgin because my body belongs entirely to me. And I have chosen not to have children, thank you. You can't even prove this thing is mine. I certainly will not give it a name. Now get out!"

Aranrhod pushed Gwydyon through the door. He descended the steep steps of her sea castle clutching the infant. The women he passed noted a strange clicking that issued from his forehead just above his bushy eyebrows. This was the sound of Gwydyon's big brain at work. When his mind churned, it did so noisily, because Gwydyon was a god of science. Had there been such gadgets in those long-ago days, the linear efforts of Gwydyon's gray matter would have resembled a clock's.

Gwydyon clicked and mused, mused and clicked and rocked the cradle with his foot. The lad had to have a name. Tick-tocking toward an idea, Gwydyon made a note to himself to remember that when he had the power, he would dispense with all matriarchal laws. There would be a New Order. Uncle Math had started the process of social change, and Gwydyon would finish it.

The child, meanwhile, was growing at a startling rate. Within weeks he had outgrown his cradle. In the few brief months it took Gwydyon to hatch a scheme to trick Aranrhod, her nameless son had already celebrated his seventh birthday.

Gwydyon glamoured a sturdy little ship from bracken and seaweed and set sail to his sister's castle by the sea, boy in tow.

Disguised as a maker of marvelous shoes and gambling on the cold drafts and chilly stone floors of seaside castles, he contrived to bring his sister aboard the boat. It took some persuading, but at last she arrived to try on a pair of toasty sheepskin slippers. And looking up from her lacings, Aranrhod saw the shoemaker's child shoot a golden wren from the sky. As he raised his little arms and aimed his miniature bow and arrow at the bird, light seemed to shimmer all around him like a halo. He so resembled the sun that Aranrhod exclaimed in amazement and called him Llew of the Skillful Hand.

Thus Gwydyon's boy was named.

And Aranrhod's anger was indescribable.

It was merely a matter of a few more months before Llew Skillful Hand had reached the age of fourteen, when boys are ready for their rites of manhood. But according to that old bugaboo, matriarchal law, manhood could only be conferred when a mother armed her son. In other words, a boy became a man when his mother said so. Perhaps if the mother were dead, a grandmother, aunt or older sister could stand in, but Aranrhod was quite alive. Too much so for Gwydyon's taste.

He retreated to his clicking and musing. It didn't take long for him to conjure an illusion of warships ready to assault Aranrhod's castle. Terror overcame the women in the household as the ships approached, for they had no defense. Again disguised, Gwydyon and Llew arrived by land just in the nick of time and pretended to offer assistance.

Aranrhod could not have been more grateful and gracious. She brought arms and with her own hand dressed the boy in sword and armor, helmet and shield.

The illusion of warships evaporated from the horizon. Aranrhod was fooled again.

And fit to be tied.

"You continue to try to force me into a motherhood I don't want! You persist in violating my autonomy!" Aranrhod raged on and on while Gwydyon laughed at her.

She tossed copper chamber pots and hurled brass plates and bronze vases at Gwydyon's head. He ducked and laughed. She shrieked and yelled. Yet she could not help but notice, through the black blaze of her anger, that Llew was a fine boy. Quiet, handsome, virile and agile. Not too clever yet, and a bit too dominated by Gwydyon— but who wasn't? Had she not been in such a righteous stew about the question of self-determination, Aranrhod might have considered Llew a young man any mother would be proud of.

But the point remained: Aranrhod did not wish to be a mother.

Llew stood innocently by, observing the scene: his mother's tantrum and Gwydyon's mocking. For all he'd been told that Aranrhod was a monster, an abnormal woman and an obstacle to his happiness, Llew felt some sympathy and admiration for her. She was large and glorious. Stubborn, forthright and independent. She positively glowed. If she showed a bad temper, well, hadn't she been tricked twice? Llew noted how strong and proud his mother was compared to the mincing maids Gwydyon occasionally brought home for pleasure or the miserable, insipid virgins Math used for furniture.

Suddenly, Aranrhod stopped her stamping and throwing and shrieking and yelping. She took a deep breath and spoke

*in a voice of such cold, hard menace, even Gwydyon gulped in
mid-guffaw and shuddered.*

*"Since you are so determined to steal women's sovereignty,
I now swear a fate upon the boy," Aranrhod growled.*

*"Llew Skillful Hand will never have a wife of the race that
is on Earth today." And here the story of Blodeuwedd begins.*

The task of creating a woman was far more complicated
than Gwydyon's usual glamouring tricks.

Even more difficult would be to shape one who bore no
resemblance whatsoever to Aranrhod. She must be compli-
ant, submissive and manageable, with no will or ambition beyond the attendance of Llew. She must perceive and fulfill
his wishes even before he'd wished them. Obviously, Gwydyon
needed help.

Math the Magician resembled a gluttonous frog sitting on his
throne, swollen legs resting in the lap of his current virgin.

"It won't be easy," he said, and Gwydyon's overstressed brain
clicked wildly.

"Pipe down, please, I'm concentrating." Math dug his heel
into the crotch of his maiden ottoman and rested his chins in
his plump, bejeweled hand. His tongue flicked in and out and

his huge, popped eyes rolled back in his head. At last, he opened them and grinned.

"Go pick the flowers of the Oak, Meadowsweet and Broom," he told Gwydyon. "And plenty of them. We want a well-endowed *morwyn*."

An odd request, not for what it was but for what it omitted. The divine essence of flowers runs through every woman's veins and is passed from womb to womb. Each woman carries within her the endlessly renewing spirit of Iris for wisdom, Heather to protect against violence, Raspberry to ease the pain of childbirth, Hyacinth to relieve grief, Foxglove for a strong heart, Lily for unconditional love, Rose for healing and the sight, Cowslip for wantonness and pleasure, Huckleberry for prophetic dreams, Loosestrife for peace, Mugwort for authority, Moss for prosperity, Marigold for freedom and, to understand the language of the birds, Lilac for its own dear sake and more.

The bouquets of feminine power are the stuff of constant creation. Yet none of these were included in Math's prescription, for this was to be a woman conceived and ripened outside the womb with plants that are metaphysically masculine.

"We are manufacturing an ideal creature in our own image," the magician reminded his nephew. "Why muck up the works with female particulars? We've got Meadowsweet for love and happiness, and that's enough emotion to guarantee that Llew's new wife will adore him. Now let's get to work!"

They began, of course, with Oak, for no sentient being can be formed without the primordial tree of perfect speech, greatest intelligence, metamorphosis and transformation. Carefully pouring acorns, leaves, bark and petals into a huge cauldron, they tossed and folded until the elements of the plant were thoroughly blended. They added two bushels of the Meadowsweet, nine handfuls of yeast, a liter of cow's milk, four dozen eggs, three cups of honey and a bucket of their own urine and spit and whipped the mixture into a peck and a half of finely chopped Broom.

Math and Gwydyon muttered their spells and sifted the finest porcelain powder into the blossoms. They stirred and poked and kneaded and pinched. Till at last, she came into focus.

And they named the woman lying on their wizard-slab, inert as a furloughed puppet, Blodeuwedd.

The proud parents sprinkled Blodeuwedd with water and sheep's blood. The florets, foliage, buds, seeds, pollen and wilted petals unfolded and burst into life.

She sat up and stared with rare eyes, white and violet as the Meadowsweet, languid and heavy as drooping stems in early summer. She smiled at Math and Gwydyon, meek and malleable, bright as the evergreen Broom on a snowy heath.

"Papa," Math crooned, pointing to himself and Gwydyon.

"Papa," Blodeuwedd repeated.

"Let's validate the experiment," Gwydyon suggested.

She passed every exam (gentle, easy tests, for Blodeuwedd had, after all, just been born). Through each trial, request and instruction, she was relentlessly nice, remorselessly genial, submissive, acquiescent and daughterly.

"Just to be sure Aranrhod hasn't pulled any of her bossy witchery on us, let's conclude with the wand-leaping test," said Math, eyeing Gwydyon, and Gwydyon glanced back at Math, each briefly suspicious of the other until they remembered that neither had yet been alone with the girl.

The wand never quivered but lay still as a stick.

The next day, they married Blodeuwedd to Llew.

No one compared with Blodeuwedd. None could look at her without sad sighing, without feeling acutely his or her own withering youth and beauty. The other women at the wedding feast were somehow unable to open their hearts to this motherless piece of perfection. In Blodeuwedd's presence they became muddled and uprooted.

Llew was glad to have a wife and all the amenities that accompanied his new social status. From named boy to armed man, he had graduated to married landowner, a young patriarch with choice property and a castle of his own, given to him by Uncle Math. Llew knew nothing except what he'd been taught by Gwydyon. Yet as he stood beside his gorgeous, demure bride, his mind turned to Aranrhod. Was Blodeuwedd not more of an object than a woman? Then again, she seemed to mirror Llew; she was his gynandrous double. He shook off his shyness, pushed his mother's image from his mind, puffed up his chest, faced his bride and settled into marriage as he was expected.

It was not altogether difficult. In bed, Llew found Blodeuwedd tractable and docile. Had he been more experienced in love, he might have sensed that she was somehow absent, as if the Oak were still at work, continuing its transformation. Yet she was sultry and torpid as honey and milk, a passive partner with whom Llew had no clear reason to be disgruntled.

Day after day, Blodeuwedd performed the job for which she'd been fabricated. The Broom provided her with soldierly obedience and tenacity, as well as housewifely industry. In fact, her clean and orderly home was the envy of all.

And although Gwydyon perceived a lack of chemistry between Llew and his bride, the god of science pushed all doubts from his mind, choosing instead to be satisfied with his custom-built daughter-in-law, who met every qualification he and Math had ever dreamed of in a woman.

So time passed uneventfully. Llew prospered. Gwydyon retired to his experiments and noisy ruminations and there was not a peep out of Aranrhod. Only Math was unhappy, as virgin after virgin deserted him, and the acceptable *morwyn* grew younger and younger.

As ever in spring, the daffodils and narcissus returned and Llew Skillful Hand left Blodeuwedd to go hunting. She watched him ride out, smooth and fresh and fair, bright and shining as daybreak. She waved and blew kisses until he disappeared over the horizon. Then she turned briskly to her wifely duties, organizing the servants for the planting, milking, cheese making, scrubbing and bread baking. She took up her weaving by a window. She was perennially pleasant, neither happy nor sad.

Evening fell, and as Blodeuwedd ordered the tallows lit, she heard the sound of hunting horns. She was mildly surprised that Llew was back so soon. He was never unlucky in the hunt and stayed the course until exhaustion demanded his return. It did not occur to Blodeuwedd to worry that Llew might have suffered some injury. As happiness and sorrow had been neglected in her manufacture, so had anxiety.

Blodeuwedd put on her prettiest gown and poured a cup of ale with which to meet her husband at the door. But instead of Llew, there stood another fellow, who looked her up and down with astonishment—as all men did. Blodeuwedd thought nothing of it.

"I am Goronwy the Staunch, Lord of Penllyn," the man stuttered. Her loveliness had rendered him breathless. "My men and I have been hunting near this castle and we seek a resting place for the night."

Goronwy was stout and graying and his features looked as if they had traveled many places. He was not handsome and glowing like Llew; rather, he was so ugly as to be magnificent. Whereas Llew recalled a sunny day, Goronwy brought forth visions of a hoary mountain tempest. His face was crusty as bark, and black stubble dotted his chin like lichen. He was cousin to the gnarled Oak, and the sap in Blodeuwedd's veins exploded with recognition.

She shoved the alehorn into his hands and squeezed her eyes. She imagined her tongue playing in the large gap between Goronwy's teeth. Imagination was unfamiliar to her and it frightened her.

She pulled herself together and curtsied the stranger through the door.

"The gods know we will be disgraced for letting this chieftain go elsewhere at this hour and not asking him in," she told the servants. She sent them to fetch water for his bath and prepare a supper.

Blodeuwedd's heart crashed and thumped. While Goronwy bathed, she ran to her looking glass and pulled her hair up this way and down that and braided it and twisted it with ribbons. She fussed and fumed and shoved at her ample cleavage and smeared it with powdered rose petals and paced the floor and whispered "Mine! Mine!" and knew not what she said, for she had never wanted anything or anyone before in her short life.

They dined alone and Blodeuwedd was radiant. She glanced shyly at Goronwy with her Meadowsweet eyes and batted her lashes and sucked slowly and seductively at strings of meat. He could not stop staring at her until, at last, he made bold to place his hand on her knee and she reached down and guided it up her skirts and soon they were kissing and fumbling and stumbling to her bedchamber.

Blodeuwedd came alive. The Oak had reached its pitch. Blodeuwedd chose Goronwy, and by her choice, her humanity emerged. Half-baked and presented to Llew as the chef d'oeuvre of men's ideals, she had been tame and biddable. For the first time, her flesh tingled like true skin, at once pliant and solid. Her slavish, sluggish sheep's blood—toxified by male urine and spit—now stormed wildly, clean and fierce as a waterfall. And although Goronwy, caressing every inch of her body, muttered again and again of Blodeuwedd's perfection, she felt gloriously imperfect. Marvelously real.

But when it was over, a bitter taste crept into Blodeuwedd's mouth. The sour taste of marital tyranny. The terrible knowledge that she was disposable, a pretty pawn in Gwydyon's game. And somewhere deep in Blodeuwedd's bones, the belligerence and stamina of Broom began to stir.

The next day, Goronwy rose to leave, but Blodeuwedd clung to him and begged him to stay. He could not resist. They slept together that night and the next and the next, and Blodeuwedd could not get enough. The days with Goronwy passed in long talk. No longer was Blodeuwedd indifferent. She expressed opinions; she had ideas; she laughed. She discovered passion, foolishness and friendship. Finally, she confessed her origins and told Goronwy that with or without him, she wanted nothing more than to be fully a woman. Goronwy was of the old school of matriarchal law, and Blodeuwedd's story offended him, for Gwydyon's tampering was an offense against Nature. He embraced and comforted her as she wept. They gazed at each other and there was no part of them that did not feel love.

Thus, on the night before Llew was expected home, Goronwy made this suggestion to Blodeuwedd: she must discover how Llew could be killed, for he was a child of the goddess and it would be no easy task to get rid of him. She did not balk, for killing Llew, she knew, would be her only path to freedom.

Goronwy the Staunch returned to Penllyn, and Llew returned home to an apparently happy wife. Her voice was louder, she was more talkative and even witty. He had never seen her be anything but deferential and even-tempered, but now and then he noticed a darkness pass over her face which reminded him of Aranrhod. She seemed less and less a feminine duplicate of himself, and thus he wanted her more and more.

One night, soon after Llew's return, Blodeuwedd turned to him and said, "I have had nightmares, horrible omens. Your absence this time was long and caused me to fret and dream of your death. I beg you, dear one, tell me how you can be killed so that I can protect you and sleep soundly."

It did not occur to Llew to mistrust Blodeuwedd. She had

been created by his father for his own pleasure, and Gwydyon, in Llew's estimation, did not make mistakes and would never betray him. In the second instance, Llew was right. Gwydyon loved his boy above all possessions.

So Llew curled into Blodeuwedd's arms—arms that had been shaped especially for him—and said, "Don't worry, my love. I can't be killed indoors or out-of-doors or on a horse or on foot."

"Well, then," Blodeuwedd sighed, "you can't be killed at all."

"Ah, but I can," he laughed, and told her that in order for him to die, he must be on the bank of a river with one foot on the back of a billy goat and the other on the rim of a tub in which a bath had been prepared for him. The spear that could kill him would take a year to make. It could be carved, polished and sharpened only during full moons.

The next day, Blodeuwedd sent a trusted messenger to Goronwy. He worked the spear until it was perfect, and at the end of a year, he sent word back to Blodeuwedd that all was ready.

"My lord," Blodeuwedd said to Llew one night over dinner, "I am thinking of what you told me and how it might come about. If I prepare the bath, will you show me how you might stand on the goat and the edge of the tub? It seems a mean feat, indeed an impossible feat, and I need reassurance that you cannot do it and are therefore in no danger."

Llew was proud. Gwydyon had spoiled and pampered him,

and while he had a certain sweetness, too, he was a show-off, vain as high noon.

He not only agreed, he prodded Blodeuwedd to hurry while he flexed his biceps and stretched and strutted.

Blodeuwedd sent for Goronwy in secret and went to prepare the bath. She found the oldest, most slothful buck in the herd. Goronwy hid, while Blodeuwedd laughed and goaded Llew.

"Now I'll see that I need not ever worry, for even you, my husband, agile as you are, cannot balance here like this."

And she bathed him and ran her hands up and down his belly and back, and when it was done and he was dripping wet, he leaped out of the tub and stood, one foot on the back of the snoozing billy goat, one foot on the rim of the tub, glowing with pride, while his penis, so recently cleaned and coddled, saluted the endeavor.

At once, Goronwy the Staunch rose to one knee and cast the spear full force at Llew and struck him in the side so that the shaft stuck out but the head stayed in. And Llew Skillful Hand gave a horrible scream and flew away in the form of an eagle and was not seen again.

Blodeuwedd and Goronwy spent happy days together—although, truth be told, there were fleeting moments when she wondered at his staunchness, his airtight manliness. Nonetheless, Blodeuwedd blossomed. Perhaps, in the gathering of Oak, Meadowsweet and Broom, detritus from the womanly blooms had drifted like weeds into her mix. She developed a smidgen of wisdom, a strong heart, a healing hand, a little insight and more. Nevertheless, she often wandered the halls of Goronwy's castle, rootless, insubstantial, fictitious.

Blodeuwedd and Goronwy lived in peace and thrived together, for Gwydyon had neither the time, the energy nor the inclination for vengeance. He was searching for Llew. Days, weeks, months and a year passed as the god of science probed and analyzed the elements, and tried every manner of alchemy to locate his precious boy. And when all that failed, he took to walking and trooped over hill and dale, beating the bushes and calling and calling for Llew Skillful Hand.

One foggy day, in despair and grieving, Gwydyon came upon a white pig whom he knew to be the sow goddess, Cerridwen, ancient, venerated Mother. She was fat, ungainly and neglected, but her eyes were stern and kind. In spite of his arrogance and impiety, his brazen violation of Nature, the sow took pity on him, for she, too, had children she loved and some she'd lost.

She led him—slowly, for by now Gwydyon was exhausted—up a stream and toward a valley, where she stopped to feed on rotten flesh and maggots that fell to the ground from a cliff. On the cliff was a nest where an eagle perched, and each time it shook, worms and rotten flesh fell away and these the sow goddess gobbled as offerings.

The raptor was golden and bright and shining, but its wing hung limp and dragging. Gwydyon suspected he was Llew. He stood beneath the cliff and raised his arms in an arch to the hazy sun and sang:

An oak grows between two lakes,
Dark sky and glen.
If I speak truly,
This comes from Llew's feathers.

Down and tissue and bits of gore fell from the eagle as it dropped from the cliff to the top of a tree below. Gwydyon sang on:

An oak grows on a high plain
Soaked by rain and putrefaction.
The oak supports the Crafts,
In its branches sits Llew Skillful Hand.

The crippled eagle dropped to the lowest branch of the tree. And Gwydyon sang again:

An oak grows on a slope,
The refuge of a handsome prince.
If I speak truly,
Llew will come to my lap.

The eagle dropped to Gwydyon's knee and the god of science struck him with his magic wand and the bird changed into human form. Llew was skin and bone and sickly and Gwydyon wrapped the hole where Goronwy's spear had entered his side and took the youth home. He fed him potions and nursed him until he was well again.

In a year's time, Llew Skillful Hand rose from his sickbed and went to Math.

"Lord, it is time to demand compensation from the man who did me this injury."

Math rumbled and farted and scratched his sole against his virgin footstool.

"And Blodeuwedd?" he asked.

"That is my lord Gwydyon's problem," Llew answered, "for he made the girl to be my plaything, but she was my wife and I came to love her, though she could not love me. I daresay she was missing some component, and that lack was neither her fault nor mine. No, my lord Math, I will take Goronwy and try to persuade Gwydyon to leave the woman alone."

But there was no persuading Gwydyon. What he had engineered, he would destroy, and his mind clicked with plans of revenge. Blodeuwedd had emerged far enough from the shadows to rebel against his authority, and now he feared her and could never forgive her.

Llew Skillful Hand gathered his forces, rode to Penllyn and surrounded Goronwy's castle. Goronwy the Staunch guided Blodeuwedd and her attendants out a secret passage that led to safety in the mountains. Then he returned to his battlements and stood his ground against Llew Skillful Hand, but Llew's warriors overcame him. Goronwy the Staunch sent messengers to ask Llew Skillful Hand if he would accept land or gold for the injury put upon him, but Llew refused.

"You must come to where I was when you cast the spear at me, while I stand where you stood, and you must let me throw a spear at you. That is the least I will accept."

So Goronwy went where Llew had been, but there was no one to bathe him before he balanced on the back of the buck goat and the rim of the tub.

Thus, he made one request: he asked that Llew allow him to put a stone between himself and the blow. And Llew agreed, but he threw the spear with such vigor and jealousy that it pierced both the stone and Goronwy the Staunch. The Lord of Penllyn died, and the stone still stands on the bank of Avon Gynvael with the spear stuck through it and so it is called Llech Oronwy.

Meanwhile, Blodeuwedd and her women ran from the castle to the mountain sanctuary. But Gwydyon, riding fast behind them, enchanted the attendants so that they could no longer travel on their feet but had to walk on their hands. When they reached the river, the women drowned, every one.

Gwydyon leaped off his horse and chased Blodeuwedd. He seized her by the hair. He spun her three times left, three times right.

Seven times he raised his hand to kill her. But he could not do it, for she was a product of his imagination.

He held her by the shoulders and shook her, as if to loosen and detach the magic, the petals and leaves and pollen and buds and seeds that fashioned her. And Blodeuwedd yielded her body like a broken branch and neither was she afraid nor did she cry out. No longer did she care whether she lived or died, for she had been truly alive only briefly and then not long enough to cultivate her soul.

"I will not kill you!" Gwydyon screamed. "I will do worse. I will let you go in the shape of a bird to punish you for the shame you have brought upon Llew Skillful Hand. Never will you show your face in daylight for fear of other birds. They will be hostile to you and it will be their nature to maul and molest you wherever they find you. You will eat hair, bones and gristle!"

And Gywdyon heaved Blodeuwedd high into the air. She rose, hovered and turned into an owl.

A flawless creature, soft and feathery, with muscular, soundless flight. Blodeuwedd was real at last, though still and ever banished to half-light, veiled by night. And she is still called Blodeuwedd, and Gwydyon fears her yet, for she can see in all directions. Her owlflower heart beats in harmony with the moon. She rises suddenly out of the shades, a winged vapor.

Retold from *The Mabinogion*.

BANFENNID

The Fianna were bands of roving warriors, social outsiders who joined together for various reasons, among them to avenge wrongdoing. Some were expelled from their clans or were landless, or were the sons of kings who had quarreled with their fathers. Some were temporary fennid, who, having come of age or made their points, returned in good standing to their tribes. But others, like the Rigfennid (or chief fennid) Fionn mac Cumhall, preferred to live permanently as outlaws, hunting, fishing, fighting, moving back and forth between this world and the Other, consorting with faeries and now and again acting as mercenaries on behalf of the clans. Their mode of warfare was considered honorable and lawful. In Celtic mythology, there are several examples of banfennid, female outlaws. Imbolc, now Candlemas, took place on February 1; Beltane on April 30 and May 1; Lughnasad on August 1; and Samhain on November 1. Yule occurs on or near the winter solstice.

I
Criedne

A yellow torch above the Earth. An angry, scorched light. I stay one day ahead of the Moon.

Once I lived in a beautiful village, in the house of my father, Conall Blackfoot. Music and gaiety, ale poured freely, the bards sang long of our clan's honor, and many nights we danced. My father grinned at the merriment from his high seat.

I danced. A motherless maiden, yet full of childish joy. I danced and sang by the gleam of a hundred stone lamps burning with peat which caught the light of gems encrusted in my skirt. The shadows of my boots hopped and quaked like leaves. The boys twirled me in circles and whirled from girl to girl. The bronze beads on my shawl jingled and jangled. And the ribbons in my loose hair gently slapped my pretty teeth whenever I tossed my head.

When the crocus shoves its beak through snow-damp soil, when day equals night and Lugh Sungod crosses the starry seam, we danced and sang to the feasting and clapping of nobles and crones and churls. As we jigged and shouted, a cold and wicked wind lashed through the hall. The hearth and all the hundred lamps blew out. Girls giggled and boys grunted. The druids bawled frantic spells against sorcery.

While the household fumbled and chattered and yelled in the dark, someone grabbed me from behind. Pushed me to the dirt floor. Thrust his tongue into my mouth and rammed his penis between my knees and up and up my thighs it crawled and into me. He heaved and moaned. I struggled. I kicked and bit and wriggled and tried to snap my legs shut, but he was large and too strong for me. And it was too dark to see him.

At last, someone found fire to light the stone lamps. The tiny flames flickered. First one and two, then twenty, fifty, then a hundred, and the hall was bright again. But he was gone. And I lay sobbing on the floor. The other girls huddled helplessly over me. None had seen a thing. My father strode to my side and pulled me upright.

Don't weep, Criedne. The daughter of Conall Blackfoot has no fear of the dark.

He summoned a servant to take me to my bedcloset and she undressed me, folded my torn skirt and washed the blood from my thighs. She stroked my hair and rubbed my back with her raw hands until I slept.

Nine months to the day, I gave birth to a son. I called him Glas mac Criedne, son of Criedne, for his begetter was invisible.

A child of the dark, born at Yule, the shortest day, when dark is dark indeed.

The druids clucked their tongues with anxious disapproval. In grim silence and with a bitter nod, my father welcomed Glas mac Criedne into his household. Although I was thirteen winters old and still a maid for never having loved willingly, I would not join the boys and girls to dance again until Imbolc.

On Brigit's day, I bound my waist with a straw rope, for the Divine Mother and her sisters, Brigits three, surround and guard the belly. I sang the dawn hymns at the holy well.

Early on Brigit's morn,
The serpent will come from the hole.
I will not molest the serpent,
Nor will the serpent molest me.

My father and I bent together to drink from the spring. At Imbolc, the waters anoint and bless cursed women and cure the laxity in men.

Three things renew the world:
A woman's womb,
a cow's udder
and a blacksmith's forge.

The nine Daughters of Flame, who tend Brigit's sacred beacon, filed round the fire, hidden by hoods of purple fleece. They marched into the smithy chanting and sprinkling the holy water and round and round the rowan they went. Boys and girls, men and women followed, wearing garlands and brooches of shamrock—three fresh green hearts of three kind goddesses—and the dancers clacked scalloped shells in time to the harp and flute and drum.

Into the hall we proceeded. Skipping round and round the hearth. We lit the hundred lamps and drank the warm ewe's milk, a feast of lactation and torches to midwife the light. And I, caught up in the mirth, was set moving, skirts flailing about my ankles, faster and faster, dancing in threes, spinning in frenzied encouragement of spring's labors.

At midnight, as the threesomes grew fewer and slower, a cruel wind dashed through the hall, and again, the lamps blew out. I shuddered and backed against the wall, crouched, clutched my knees, sensing hot breath plunging toward me. And that hand grabbed me again. Again, he threw me to the ground and violated me. The hair on his thighs, the swing of his testicles, the quick brutality with which he used me . . . the grunts and groans and sighs were those of the same man, the unseen father of my son.

At last, the druids relit the lamps and retreated, shaking their heads at the terrible wind that had invaded our feasts and doused the fires and that they now declared had begotten a son on the king's daughter. This time, I restrained my sobs and held my head high.

Nine months to the day, I bore another son. I called him Runtar mac Criedne. A second child of the dark, welcomed in grudging silence by my father, while the druids cast spells around the babe.

Children of the wind, untimely harbingers. O merciful deities, reveal to us the meaning of these births.

And I did not dance again.

On Beltane, my father married. Aoife came from the north from the blustery island of Iona. Boys and girls, nobles and churls, old men and crones rejoiced.

Conall Blackfoot will have sons to follow in his mighty footsteps.

My stepmother smirked at me and my two sons. And sought about the hall with squinted eyes at all the boys and men, searching for resemblances. Glancing at me, she gossiped aloud to her company of women.

I know wind. Children of the wind would be breezy and light and made of silver. These spurious whelps are solid as stones. The girl Criedne is capricious and lewd and has a secret lover. No doubt a churl whom her father would despise.

Aoife was chilly as the Scottish sea, low as the winter Sun and red as winter's bracken. Her women looked at me and laughed.

The druids watched me, too, and mumbled charms to repel the ill-conceiving wind. I pretended not to notice while we hung flowers on the doors and strewed blossoms along a spiral path of pine boughs. May color settled on every hill, and the ocean was falling to sleep. The cuckoo called. Blackbirds sang a throaty tune to the coming of summer. With horse races and games, the vigor of men and boys began to flourish. The druids lit two fire pits at dusk—one to dispatch the old and one to bring in the new—and women drove the cattle round the flames. Surely the dark season's rough wind had gone, for the woods were ruffled with soft, young green. How happy the wild birds, the timid, frail creatures singing with mad ardor while I was trapped in frightening thoughts of a spectral ravisher.

I dressed in lovely robes to make my father proud at his wedding feast. Bare white arms. A green silk frock with gold embroidery of delicate deer designs. A lavender cloak and a golden comb that held daffodils tangled in my tumbling hair.

Boys and girls, men and women ran to and fro leaping over the fires, rushing into the woods to be alone. Conall and Aoife laughing somewhere in the heavy shadows. I refused to jump the flames. Men and boys looked at me with yearning, but I cringed and shook my head at their advances. I watched, wondering which was the rapist and how to ferret him out, how to make visible the wind.

I hovered. Planning. The Beltane flames whipped the sky, then sputtered to embers in the cavernous night. I crept through the blackest black before dawn, through the snores and sighs, across the lawn to the cooling fire pit and rubbed my hands in water and then in ashes.

The rosy flush of cinders gave life to my feet. I danced now, hoping to entice him. Slowly, slowly, teetering and wobbling, while the others, even the druids, slept. I danced to a song in my head, fueled by the rhythms of the bubbling ash. Twirling, humming aloud by fits and starts to give courage to my cunning. And then someone, not a draft but a man dense as iron, hurled me down in the darkness and mounted me and penetrated me.

Instead of struggling, I flattened my hands on his back and imprinted him with soot. The wind howled and the Sun rose, awakening the others. I walked along the rim of the eerie wood, across the lawn. Couples stumbled and staggered from their trysting places. Aoife's eyes opened and she lay stretching, satisfied, smiling to herself. Men and boys shared a cold joint of roasted pig to break their fasts.

I strolled, feigning nonchalance but inspecting each man's back, each boy's shoulder blades.

Two gray handprints were pressed into the linen shirt of a tall and muscular man. An overpowering man, regal and battleworn. I did not want him to turn. And when he did, his grin was all paternal benevolence. The tough grin that had charmed me from the day I was born.

I screamed and screamed and the world danced before my eyes, fractured as if I were drowning. A dance of heartbreak, a dance against debauch. I attacked Conall Blackfoot with my fists and the servants held me back. He smiled at my attack, a secret, conspiratorial smile that only I noticed. I kicked and yowled until I was breathless and blue and swooning.

He denied it. Before druids and nobles. He blamed the wind and magic. But my handprints told the truth, and finally, he blamed me. I had enchanted him, he said. I provoked him. I aroused him, and now, he said, he was shamed by me. And they nodded in sympathy.

My shame came nine months to the day, when I bore a third son. Although now I knew their father, these sons of mine were mine alone and I would not call them mac Conall. I named the new one Imda mac Criedne, and he was born on Imbolc, when Brigit blesses mothers. In that mercurial month, she blessed Aoife with a son. Aoife, who had fixed herself against me and mine.

Conall's shame, the issue of his lying, wanton daughter, are not welcome in my home to pollute my child and lay claim to his birthright.

She petitioned Conall and the druids and nobles.

Indeed, Criedne's children create disharmony, they have no place, no status, they do not fit in and must be expelled.

In the dark of night, Glas, Runtar and Imda were taken from my bedchamber and sent into fosterage at the outer limits of my father's rich territory. I was not told where they were sent, only that they were gone forever.

Had I been less pretty, had I been quieter, had I not so loved to dance, had my clothing been drab and my smile less winning, might my father have let me alone, been untempted by me? In my thoughts, I listed the ways I could have been responsible for the king's humiliation. But had I no right to be a winsome maiden without courting perversion?

I lay in my bed shaking with repugnance toward myself and Conall Blackfoot. That he would deny inheritance to the sons who were his grandsons. That he listened to druids and heeded pitiless, jealous Aoife and let them play upon his discomfort with no shred of compassion for me. Falsehood and greed! He was not even content with a wife! I remembered him leaning beside me before Brigit's sacred spring, drinking the waters against impotence. It was I who had cured his laxity! Again and again, I felt his savage body, hurling in and out of me in the dark.

Criedne, daughter of Conall Blackfoot, has no fear of the dark.

I dressed in warm layers of austere wool and pulled on my thickest boots. I plaited my hair tight and firm behind my back, and in the dark of the night, I stole away from my father's house.

Across the weeks, Criedne wandered through wilderness, into the duns and cooking places of the Fianna. When she told her story, their indignity was roused. They taught her to fight remorselessly and hunt unawed, to run soundlessly, to render herself invisible, to love danger and memorize the twelve poetic forms. They united behind her until she had acquired three bands, each with nine grim-visaged warriors.

She led them to the northern reaches of her father's land. There she first made known her boiling power and tested her strength. Clashing, billowing, slashing and cutting, the Fianna of Criedne pillaged Conall Blackfoot's territory. They built a cairn to mark the sacking of villages and farms. They left the women and children with a message for Conall to return the birthright of Criedne's sons lest all his people and property be devastated.

She led the Fianna south, chased by Conall's warriors. Criedne turned to meet them head-on. They were helpless before the fury of Criedne Banfennid, who left but one of Blackfoot's men alive to carry a challenge to the king to fight the Fianna of Criedne in person, father and daughter one on one, or against her greatest champion.

They erected a pillar stone after the battle to commemorate their victory, and galloped away with many trophy heads.

Conall replied by sending more fighters to die at Criedne's hands.

In the west, the Banfennid at last discovered the fosterage of her three sons, Glas, Runtar and Imda, who were growing big and hardy. They did not recognize her, and Criedne wept when she held them, then grew more ferocious, more determined to return them to their proper kindred, their rightful heritage. She left them in the safety of the fosterage and destroyed all but the clan that cared for them.

Then Criedne Banfennid sent a third message to her father with promises to leave the land be and leave the clans in peace and kill no more of his warriors if he would agree to her terms. But again no answer came and Criedne sent a group of women to curse Aoife that the lips of her labia would be in conflict and strike against each other until they rotted. And Criedne's women stood outside the gates of Conall's fortress and made a Word Battle and their satire withered Aoife's gossiping women speechless.

The Fianna of Criedne set sail for her stepmother's home and pirated on land and sea until Aoife's people sent an envoy to Conall Blackfoot pleading for compromise.

Nothing could stop her. Criedne Banfennid won every skirmish, every battle, raided every mile of Conall's kingdom, rumbled and rattled across the land with her band of three times nine, and every rock she struck with her sword burst into raging flame.

Seven years passed. My Fianna had ravaged Conall's kingdom. A fitting vengeance, but not enough. By now the clans had heard the story of the rape of Criedne and greeted us with feasting and poems, songs of the legend of the she-outlaw.

And Conall's tithes shrank, his treasure was drained, his army enfeebled. Occasionally, we encountered loyal stragglers anxious to do battle with us. But we quickly routed all opponents.

On Lughnasad, when the people celebrate the Festival of First Harvest and honor the Sungod, we made our way quietly into the forest outside Blackfoot's fortress. Between the wood and the clanholding there was a meadow, a clear shot.

We waited and the Fianna pestered me with worries about a night attack. It is ill luck, they said, to strike after the Sun has set. And on Lughnasad, all the more misfortune, for the Sungod will be offended that we did not enlist his aid. But darkness had been Conall's weapon and it would be mine.

Lugh of the Long Hand plummeted to Earth. Across the cloudless day, I listened to the bells, rattles, clappers and whistles echoing from inside the fortress. Conall's people held a miserly observance and the assembly was small, for my war had left scant bounty.

He is dead! He is risen! Hail Lugh Sun!

Clip-clop of drums, shrill of flutes, cacophony of harps and hymns.

99

He is dead! He is risen!
The lion passes as fire passes.
Lugh fades to sleep and the year is dying!
Behold the grain of life
Of light
That ever dies
And is ever reborn.

I pictured the leaping, stamping, hopping. The dance around a swaying strawman and the Lughnasad brides, yoked with wreaths of flowers from their lovers. The tournament ring. The games. The marriages of a year and a day. The autumn bursts of seeds. Drunken, delirious bridegrooms lighting the strawman. The blaze mirroring noon's splendor. A copulation of cakes shaped in human and animal forms piled high, belly to belly on a table. The lovers passing bites back and forth. Mouths drawn to one another like flies to honey. For seven years, I had danced only for victory and never taken a lover, for such acts repulsed me. Now, waiting in the wood, listening to the celebration, I wept in anger and sorrow, in grief and mourning for my lost youth, for the saucy, pretty maidenhood replaced by grave righteousness.

Dusk began to fall. The flames of the burning strawman receded below the horizon, following Lugh Sungod to his rest. I curled into a brief sleep.

At midnight, the Fianna woke me. The feeble ballyhoo inside the fortress had quieted. We sneaked out of the thicket. I raised my voice to a high rallying pitch, and we set our whips to the horses. The Fianna whooped and shrieked behind me. The tired night burst awake. We charged across the meadow.

We stormed the gates. Cut down the guards. One side of the house was like a blaze of flame from the clash of spears and swords, and the other like a flock of white birds from the dust of shields.

Within the hall, Conall stood unarmed beside his high seat, thumbs hooked in his belt, massive as a mountain. Druids and nobles lined up behind him. Crumbs from the Lughnasad feast were scattered about their feet, but there was no evidence of lusty bridegrooms and hearty maidens, no happy boys and girls. Aoife skulked beside the king, clutching her sons, shivering, gray and sickly, eyes vague and squinting.

I yelled at my father.

Conall Blackfoot! The mother of the children of the wind has come to claim their rights!

He did not budge. He stared at me, defiant and unblinking. I leaped toward him and pressed the point of my knife to his throat.

Aoife jabbered. Her sons cried.

I sniggered at her while Conall's servants dashed to put out fires. The Fianna did not stop them but guarded my back. The druids muttered in the king's ear. He turned his head slightly and I pressed my knife deeper into his gullet.

Accept defeat, you windy progenitor, O dearly beloved father.

The Fianna laughed. The druids nodded and the chief of them tottered forward.

The wind has proved the superior strength of Criedne and her sons. The time has come to pay the price for incest and patrimony. It is over, Conall. Accept defeat and prosperity will return.

Not an ounce of Conall Blackfoot's warrior pride was diminished, and as he spoke an old fear fluttered through me, familiar and unexorcised by time or success.

Your three sons, Glas, Runtar and Imda, will possess all the western lands into which they have gone. The lands will never be taken from them. They will have wealth, celebrity and luck in war until the Day of Doom.

It was done.

The Fianna made their beds within the fortress and soon the household was asleep. I paced the perimeter of the lawn, thinking of my sons and how I would ride to take them the news tomorrow. How I would build our own fortress on the land I had won them. How Glas and Runtar would be glad of their inheritance; how Imda would be little impressed, for he was still a little boy, just beginning his training in manhood. I thought how this war had caused me to love them. How at their births they had been unwelcome strangers, imposed upon me. How, in fighting for them, I had come to absorb motherhood and embrace them.

In the dark, my feet began to move. I rotated my arms and hugged the sky, whispering.

He is risen! All thanks to Lugh of the Long Hand.

I capered and bobbed. Shy, then bolder and bolder, reeling, hips swiveling, fingers whisking the air, belly undulating.

Someone grabbed hold of the braid at the nape of my neck. I stopped. Pinned. Panting. My heart raced.

Criedne Banfennid, you are flesh of my flesh, a warrior proud and mighty in my own image. My chosen consort. Together we are truly like god and goddess. Stay with me, love me, and your sons alone, O Criedne, will have everything, all that is mine and more if you will give yourself freely to me.

Conall Blackfoot dragged me to him. I pulled the sharp knife from my belt. I ripped open my bodice. I cut off both my breasts. Blood spilled on the late summer grass. I flung my breasts at my father.

Since you have such a taste for my body, eat these!

I ran from the fortress into the meadow and the black dark night in a torrent of gushing blood.

Conall snatched up a lamp. He followed my scarlet trail. He lurched and stumbled, slipped on my blood and fell. The light went out. The stone glowed.

There was a great, deafening howl, a terrifying screech, and a big wind roared across the terrain and lifted my father. Then it lifted me. It carried us into the sky and higher and higher we went.

The wind tossed me to the East. It tossed Conall Blackfoot to the West. I exploded into a ball of fire and molten heat, a tempest churning round the rising Sun, Lugh's fist cupped tight around me.

And my father folded into a ball of snow and ashen chill and orbited the Moon.

I traverse the sky. I stay half a world away from him. Always hiding when he comes out.

Now and again, he finds me. He crosses my path. Eclipses me. He grins at me. The Earth darkens. But I dance quickly on.

Retold from versions by Kuno Meyer, Myles Dillon, Joseph Falaky Nagy, Richard Erdoes and Alfonso Ortiz.

II
Assa/Ni Assa
(Gentle/Ungentle)

Some say she was pretty, but others don't recall it. In her old age, she struts about like a scrawny hen, like an overcooked wing, tough and brown under greasy leathers pocked with piercings from sword and spear. Her teeth are snaggled and chipped, the thread-cutting tooth knocked out in a drubbing. Her voice is hoarse from years of screaming at youth she trains for war. Her own granddaughter is the king's charioteer, and it was she who taught the girl to handle horses and ride pell-mell through pelting rocks on the battlefield.

Only a few graybeards recollect that she was named Assa. Gentle. She excelled in all the arts daughters of kings must know. Her father was Eochu, high chieftain of Ulster. He gave her twelve foster fathers to guard her and provide her all she wanted or needed. Gentle Assa did not ask for much, for not much was left to desire in such a life as she had.

ON THE EDGE OF DREAM

Two husbands she had, as well. No, not then! She was a maiden and Eochu was reluctant to let her go.

"One husband for brains and the other for brawn!" she cackles, slapping her cunt with her cupped hand. Her husbands paled beside her son, for she begot a king, Conchobar, and put her life and love into him alone.

Not many are surnamed for their mothers. There's So-and-so mac Father or So-and-so ni Father—but *her* son, who knows his father well, calls himself Conchobar mac Nessa.

She might have been thirteen. Oh, some sweet marriageable age, though she was getting on for all Eochu's delays. Everyone agreed she would be a good wife. Who wouldn't desire the favorite daughter of a wealthy chieftain? And a quiet, diligent one at that. But she was too dreamy, though dreaming befit her years.

Do you remember how she walked with her eyes lowered? Always running into posts and horses' arses, that girl. To see her now, upright and bold, you wouldn't know it. She can leap, even in her dotage, like a squirrel from branch to branch. But if she was a clever child, she kept her shrewdness hidden. Deferred to Eochu in every decision. That's a habit which promises a child any indulgence from her father. She was a wisp, soft and modest.

It was a feast day. Which one? Never mind, there are so many. Sure it was not a festival of season's change or a god's celebration, though it turned out to be auspicious. None of Eochu's druids forewarned of it, but Cathbadh must have read it in the stars. He calculates what every day will bring, and thus he turned this one to his advantage.

Eochu was detained by other business and not among the company. Gentle Assa rode to the nearby dun of one of her

foster fathers accompanied by her maidservant and a small retinue. All twelve men had come from across Ireland with their
women, whom Assa also loved. She sat with them at the head of
the table and ate and drank and laughed behind her hand. They
say her shy laughter was like the whisper of wind in birch leaves.
The old woman sits now on her throne beside Conchobar and
tosses her head, wide-mouthed, and her laughter is like the roar
of a waterfall.

They ate their fill and drank too much and fell asleep. Assa
in a bedbox painted and pounded with gold just for her. Her
maidservant curled to sleep at her feet. Outside, the druid Cathbadh camped with his band of twenty-seven fennid, awaiting
the dawn.

Cathbadh dodders now. His body is bent and his fingers are
twisted and gnarled. For all his ailments, the druid's prophecies
ring truer than the chime of a finely wrought bronze flagon. He
is stationed by Conchobar's side. He warns of sorrows and fore-
tells victories. He names heroes. He wards off the satire of enemies with verse so pungent it molders them and counters the
curse. Cathbadh speaks to the gods, and their replies, conveyed
through his fetid old breath, take precedence even over Conchobar's decrees. Cathbadh's body is decrepit, but his brains are
like new and he refreshes them by conversing with wise and
brave ancients whose heads he stores in cedar chests in his
chamber.

Believe it or not, Cathbadh, too, was once young and wild as eagles. He had the Sight at birth, but whether he had a mother or was expelled from sunspots or spawned by salmon, none remember.

He grew fast, as heroes do, yet the thing that grew fastest on Cathbadh was his head. It was enormous. So big, some joked, that if ever they were to make a lime-paste brain-ball of Cathbadh's gray matter, it would be too huge to hurl.

Even then he was bald as a stone. The better to commune with spirits.

Cathbadh was not much older than Assa when he left his birthplace at Mag Inis with a band of nine unruly boys to survive in the green beyond the *tuatha*. Within the *tuatha*, Cathbadh felt confined. He announced he was becoming stupid, entombed by the sedentary laws of farmers. He was born to druidry, but grew bored with harps and cauldrons and ogham and sacrifice and counting comets and talking to trees. He longed for larger visitations from the Children of Light, divine transmissions that could only be found outside. There were secrets out there and Cathbadh could never bear to be left out of a secret. In the wilderness, he would learn to make the *fith-fath*, to shift his shape and occupy the souls of beasts and birds and fish and pebbles. He would uncover gates to the Otherworld and discover the passwords. Only on *fennidecht* could he satisfy his yearning for greater community with Earth's skin and Sky's mind. A year went by, and another, then another, until Cathbadh's Fianna grew to nine times three.

When the sun rose, Assa awoke and climbed out of bed. She picked her way over the snoring bodies of foster fathers, old and young and in-between, scattered here and there, asleep wherever the mead overtook them. She wrapped herself in skins and went into the wood alone to relieve herself.

She wandered a bit, eyes lowered, fascinated as ever by whatever lay on the ground. Then she meandered back to the dun, where she found her twelve fosterers and her retinue dead or writhing toward death, in puddles of blood and gore. Barely awake, they had met a challenge at the door and stumbled out to fight and lose. And the head of the eldest fosterer—a smith who forged blades so thin and sharp they could probe the thickest ethers—had been sliced clean from his neck and his sword was gone, too.

The women wailed and trembled within the house. Assa floundered from one dead foster father to the next, but her tears and cries would not bring them back.

Assa rode swiftly home with her maidservant. Her tears, they say, soaked the servant and flooded the path, and there were so many tears, so bitter and salty, the cattle and deer lick that dirt to this day, though only a coward would hunt there for easy prey.

She slid from her mount and ran into her father's hall at Emain Macha. He was breaking fast with his wives. Sleep still scabbed their eyeballs.

He was pleased to see her, then shocked. His Assa. Gentle girl. Streaking into the hall, red-faced and swollen, hair unbound and feet unshod, tripping and blundering and weeping. He stepped down from his seat to grab her. He shook her shoulders to sort the words that hiccuped from her mouth in great, spitting sobs, until, at last, he had the story.

He sat back down with a heavy sigh. Revenge she wanted, and he wanted to give it to her, for he would give her anything. Besides, had the twelve foster fathers not been boon companions of his own? Had he not chosen them especially for his precious girl? But he could not avenge them, for no one recognized the killers.

"Wait, my Assa," he pleaded. "Calm yourself. We do not know who slaughtered them, and until we do, there is nothing but air to track down."

"Do you refuse me, Father?" And for once Assa looked straight at Eochu.

"Yes," he answered. "Did you not hear the reason why? Were you not listening, daughter?"

Assa changed. Right before Eochu's eyes. Before her father's eyes and all the assembled company, and none will forget it.

She backed away. Gritted her teeth. She sneered and scowled.

"Never again call me Assa! The gentleness is dead in me. As of this moment, I am Ni Assa, the Ungentle. If you will not avenge my fosterers, I will!"

She stormed from the hall, ripping off her garments as she went. Naked, she stood before her father's house, facing a growing crowd, and shouted. No one had ever heard her raise her voice. Her eyes were raised, too, eyeballs rolled back. She ranted and raved. She snarled ugly satires on her invisible enemy. She called for men to follow her.

110

Do you recall the plundering? The Banfennid Nessa was merciless. She took hostages and questioned them with beatings and threats. "Which is the Fianna that killed my fosterers in the dun that morning?" "Who perpetrated this crime?"

Her widowed foster mothers succored Nessa, for the more ruthless she became, the further into outlawry her Fianna drifted. The foster mothers, too, wanted vengeance, and they still cared for Ni Assa's well-being. The fosterer is enjoined to the child for life. They rubbed balm on her wounds and lotions on her skin to smooth it, but Nessa's brown, hard, exposed flesh could not be tenderized back to its former delicacy and fairness.

It was the eldest foster mother, the smith's widow, who gave Nessa her sword. Took it down from the hook on the wall, where the smith had kept it. Some say the sword was also a key to the Otherworld, and this is how Nessa was ambushed.

She is a merry, daft one now, that old queen. She gets her way. Where her father once coddled her, now it's her son. On *fennidecht*, she learned arrogance and obstinacy—lessons not far from the surface of a girl as well cosseted as Assa had been—and with time and age, she learned cunning, too. You can see it in her yet. She's a fox, that wily old woman.

Nessa Banfennid slept on the grass. She hunted and fished for food. She sat cross-legged by the cooking pits telling stories and verses. She played sporting games and engaged in contests of strength, and practiced until she beat nearly all her opponents. She stared at men directly. Maiden no longer, she took lovers from among her Fianna. Sometimes, she got information from a handsome hostage by bribing him with the friendship of her thighs. How she loves these days to brag of *that*!

Eochu paced and paced for days, horrified that his Gentle One had followed the roaming, lawless path of the fennid. He tried to stop her. He sent warriors with orders not to touch a hair on her head but to return her whole and healthy to Emain Macha. She laughed at her father's troops and emissaries, then plundered on, seeking the killers of her twelve fosterers and finding pleasure in freedom itself. Anyone with eyes can see she never resumed her unassuming ways but takes her liberties as she pleases, heedless of the rules that bind us.

Not too many months passed before she figured it was Cathbadh who had done the deed. She pursued him hard, and evenly matched they were, too, both with nine times nine Fianna. How did he elude her? How is it *she* did not capture him, but *he* her?

It must have been an hour in the day when the worlds open ever so slightly to each other so that spirits can slip through. Nessa undressed and stepped into a lake to bathe. She splashed and paddled like a hound. She floated and turned circles like an otter. She dived and followed the stream under water like a trout. And when she came up for breath and looked to the shore, there was a man. Well, hardly a man, more an overgrown boy with an uncommon big head, holding her sword and pointing it at her with one hand, turning it slowly as if unlocking an invisible door. His other hand beckoned her with a crooked finger. He muttered and mumbled all the while.

"Hah! It's Cathbadh!" she yelled. "Ho, druid! Is your head upside down?"

She loves to tell the story to annoy him, for when Cathbadh was a fennid, he'd grown a beard.

She dipped backward to wet her hair and shot water from her mouth. Then, the way she tells it, she laughed at him. Laughed uproariously, rubbing her head to mimic his hairless noggin and sticking her tongue out.

Unflappable, then as now, Cathbadh continued to summon Nessa with that waggling finger. He stood in an enchanted place between her and her weapon. He recited poem after poem. He held all the power in that sword and those words.

Water rose around her as up the sides of a cup. She was trapped in a vessel of water. Water encased her, bound her arms and dragged her to shore; weeds caught in her hair, silt gushed between her toes. The lake drew her to him, receded and left her spellbound standing before him. He pressed the flat of her own blade between her breasts, the tip of it against her throat.

"Make peace with me, Nessa," he demanded.

"And how should I do that, murdering egghead?" she gurgled, water dripping from her lips.

"Lie down with me here," he said.

"You have my weapon. You can make me do anything, and I will buy my life, for I like it. Do you think lying with you will truly bring peace?"

"I will beget a son on you," he said. "A king upon a queen." He flicked the blade and drew a tiny drop of blood. He wiped the blood with his finger and licked it.

She lay down. Wouldn't anyone? She admits she was "druided," she says, by his mutterings and his magic, but the old woman will die before she owns that she was afraid.

And he, with the weapon still pressed between her breasts, lay on top of her, and when it was done, he told her they were husband and wife by one of the ten forms of marriage, the form of force.

"You knew I *could* have killed you, did you not?" she asked. The old woman still cannot admit defeat.

"I did," Cathbadh said, but if he spoke true or was only appeasing her, no one but he knows.

"Why did you kill my fosterers?"

"It was rash and done in wildness. I went there to capture you. To take you. But you were nowhere to be found and the fosterers performed their fostering duties as they should. They fought for you. I won."

Nessa sighed. What could have been so enticing in the wood that she had stayed there with lowered eyes, shuffling in awkward circles that early morning? She would gladly have gone with Cathbadh to save the lives of her fosterers.

"Will you meet the claims of my foster mothers for killing their husbands? Will you compensate them as befits their status?"

"If not I," Cathbadh said, "then our son."

Cathbadh sent Nessa to fetch water from the lake. The sorcery had made him thirsty. There were two worms in the cup and he told her to drink it herself. In two brave gulps, she swallowed the worms.

"I did what he ordered," the old queen sniffs, "but only because I knew that doing so betokened a marvelous child. . . . Besides, the bald coot had me druided."

She trailed along behind him, not gentle but acquiescent, for he had wrapped her in a charm she could not escape and that made her obey. They did not leave *fennidecht* too soon, but in nine months' time, with Nessa heavy and dragging her feet, they set across the plain of Muirthemne to meet with Eochu.

It was on a flagstone by the river Conchobar that Nessa's birth pangs came on. While Nessa labored, Cathbadh recited poems of mighty births that had come before and prophecies of the illustrious future of the child about to be born.

"He charged out of my womb, clutching a worm in each hand as a sign of his greatness," the old queen says, smacking her cunt and cuffing her son.

"His entrance into the world was as daring as his life has been. He plunged head over heels out of the womb, into the water. Cathbadh seized him, pulled him out, put him to my breast and named him for the river. My son is like that river," Nessa boasts. "He is wide, strong and quick. He washes easily over every obstacle in his path."

Nessa, Cathbadh and the child Conchobar returned to Eochu, who gave them vast lands and made Cathbadh chief druid of Emain Macha. A strange reward for killing Eochu's boon companions. But Eochu wanted to settle his daughter, to have her near, and not even kings can dispute the ten forms of marriage, or any of our laws.

But Eochu demanded immediate justice for the murdered fosterers, and Cathbadh provided generous compensation, beyond the customary, to all their wives and children.

Some wondered why Nessa—though she disbanded her Fianna and returned to the *tuatha*—refused to give up her warrior ways. Her prancing and sword-swinging, her battling, bragging and sporting games.

That has an easy answer.

"It makes me sick to think of Assa," she says. "A cowardly half-wit, veiled and pappy, submerged in gentleness. Had Assa raised her eyes, the fosterers would not have died!"

And Nessa kept her weapons close by to support her ambitions for her son. It was prophesied that he would be glorious. She would see to it.

Peace they got, but not for long. The birth of Conchobar began to break the spell that bound Nessa to Cathbadh. Rearing the child snapped her out of it. All she could think of was him. She picked his fosterers with care so the boy would have potent allies. She trained him herself. She taught him to wield her own sword, which, in his hands, stretches long as a rainbow.

Within their house, Nessa and Cathbadh fought on, and many remember the arguments, the shrieking, the tossing of vessels and clashing of daggers.

"I could not love him," the old queen chortles, patting the ancient druid on his wrinkled head. "Nor live with such tremendous brains and blathering oracles that spoiled every tale."

At that, Cathbadh shakes his chins and smiles at her. For all the affection time and old age bring, beneath the bright eyes Nessa turns on the druid, can you not see the spite she harbors toward him?

Cathbadh's spell dissolved as the child grew. Nessa came more and more to her Ni Assa self again. She threw his belongings out the door. "One of the three forms of divorce!" she snorts. His cauldrons and carved stones, his harp and his bags of herbs flew out the house. The cedar chests burst open and heads rolled and scattered. Some swear they recognized the dried, shrunken faces of their own ancestors.

When Eochu died, struck in the temple by an enemy's brainball, Nessa moved into the bed of his elected successor, Fergus mac Roich, whose strength is that of seven hundred men, who is tall as a giant, eats seven pigs, seven deer and seven cows and drinks seven vats of liquor at every meal. For a while, they were well matched, those two. But she would only grant her favors if he promised to let her son rule for a year.

Do you remember that just before the year was up, Nessa traveled through Ulster, now gentle, now ungentle, appealing for her son's continuing rule? Conchobar is lucky and beautiful. The land flourishes under his feet. We agreed that he could be chieftain so long as his reign is fertile. On the Rock of Kings, we mated him to the goddess and he drank from her golden goblet.

And Fergus, who preferred tippling, feasting, footling and playing chess to the mighty duties of kingship, gave in with a nod, a grin and a shrug.

Nessa sulked, for triumph came too easily.

But by that time, she was nearly the age we see her now, and content to forgo a fight.

FITH-FATH SUITE

The *fith-fath*, or, interchangeably, *fath-fith* (pronounced fee-fi), is a Celtic incantation that renders a person transformed or invisible to mortal eyes. The transformation can be voluntary or imposed. The *fith-fath* is especially useful to hunters, warriors and travelers.

I
The Hound

This, now, is the story of the fith-fath of Tuiren and the birth of Fionn mac Cumhall's cousins.

And these are the things that were dear to Fionn—
the din of battle, the banquet's glee,
the shingle grinding along the shore,
when he dragged his war boats down to sea.
The dawn wind whistling among his spears,
the magic song of his minstrels three,
the blackbird cries in the rough glen ringing
and the bay of his hounds in Letter Lee.

Now after Fionn mac Cumhall had won his slain father's place as Rigfennid of the mighty Fianna, his mother Muirne asked him to find a husband for her sister Tuiren. He could refuse Muirne nothing, but the acquisition of husbands was not among the manly skills of Fionn mac Cumhall.

And all the more difficult was his task, for Fionn's aunt was called Tuiren the Homely. Her nose was long and so was her chin. Her eyes were small, though they sparkled merrily. Her voice was sharp and startling high. She was freckled and pale and her kinky, unruly hair had a copper hue that brought to Fionn's mind the glow of his dogs' fur when they lay before the fires of the Fianna's cooking places. Yet her figure was fine and low and lean and muscular, for she loved to dance and hunt and play games of strength and precision. But Tuiren the Homely had grown in the shadow of Muirne, so that any man who may have had a passing fancy for the younger sister forgot her instantly when he saw the older, who was soothing as May blossoms.

Thus Tuiren had long ago given up wishing for the attentions so lavishly paid to her sister. Tuiren knew not the reason Muirne sent her alone to Fionn, but neither was she concerned with reasons. At her nephew's forest dun, far from sedentary settlements, she could be lighthearted as the Fianna, who kept peace with the clans and made war for them, but while the clans' deepest pleasures were in hard labor, laws and trophies, the Fianna treasured freedom.

And when Fionn laid eyes on his aunt, he despaired of his mother's request, for not only was Tuiren uncomely, she had no property. No cattle, no sheep, no pigs, no bronze for a bride-bargain.

Now Tuiren's disposition was sweet and she was quick to invent a verse. And versifying was a quality most highly prized among the talkative Fianna. It did not take Tuiren long to join their sports of footracing, spear throwing, chess and poetry. She excelled at them all, and soon she endeared herself to the Fianna, who loved her as they would a boyish sister.

Thus, when Tuiren asked to join the hunt, they let her. But they sent her with handsome Iollan, whose pride of hunters was less successful than the others. Some said Iollan was a cautious leader. Others that he was cowardly.

And Tuiren could sniff and spot the quarry even before the hounds. She stalked prey as if she were invisible. She ran and leaped ahead of the dogs, never disturbing a hair on branch or leaf or snapping twigs when her light, silent feet sped across the ground. Amid the fierce brace of hounds and hunters, she pounced on the game and sliced its throat. And returning to the dun, Tuiren laughed and jigged triumphant around the largest boar that any man had ever taken. And in that moment, Tuiren the Homely seemed beautiful even to herself.

Now Iollan took Fionn aside and asked for Tuiren. Such a woman would give him sons to outshine the best of men. And Fionn was surprised that the task he believed might be the first he could not accomplish was so easily done. And Tuiren was pleased, for no man had ever wanted her, least of all a man as handsome as Iollan.

Thus the bargain was struck. Fionn made Iollan give his word to all the Fianna, so that not a one would ever take Iollan's side. And Iollan promised that Tuiren would be returned safe if ever Fionn or Muirne asked for her. Fionn bade Iollan give sureties for himself, and this he did gladly, pledging his life, for the contract sealed him to Fionn and his closest companions.

Now Iollan had a faerie sweetheart, Uchtdealb of the Fair Breast, and she was dazzling as Tuiren was plain. Each night,

Iollan wandered from the cooking places of the Fianna, out of range of their fires and dances and songs and stories and snores, to a rock by the river where the thorny rose plaited to form a curtain across the door.

And there Iollan whistled, a whistle rounded out with the hoot of an owl. And when he had whistled thus three times, Uchtdealb came forth clothed only in golden hair that draped over her alabaster breast and that made enticing reflections on the soft mounds and heaves of her slim, tall form. Iollan drew off his robe and they spent each night tumbling on the mossy bank of the river. Till dawn, when Uchtdealb pulled away, giggling, and stepped through the rose-briar curtain, enfolded back into the Sidhe.

Thus Uchtdealb was distressed as she waited a full turn of the moon for Iollan's whistle. Night after night, there was mere cold silence till, at last, Uchtdealb floated out of the Rock of the Sidhe disguised as a shred of white fog. She seeped into Fionn's dun, past the oak that marked the great gate, and there she spied on the marriage feast of Iollan and Tuiren.

Now Uchtdealb grieved. She wailed for yet another turn of the moon beside the briar door that separates this world from the Other. And those who heard the sound shuddered and embraced their loved ones.

And when she was done weeping, the faerie put on the garments of a messenger boy and set out across the heath to Iollan's house.

Now Tuiren had not asked to join Iollan in the hunt that day. And many days had passed since she had asked. She was early with child. Her mornings were sickly and she slept fitfully, for the nights were chilly and all about the house was a dark, disturbing wail that seemed to speak her husband's name. But Iollan ignored the night cries as he was beginning to ignore Tuiren. And she hoped, soon, he would ignore her bed, for she found no satisfaction with him but lay under Iollan as if imprisoned, pinned and smothering, dreaming of woods and birds and bears and streams and the jolly company of the Fianna.

Thus she sat beside the hearth, her heart distracted and swirling with nameless desires.

Now came a knock on the door. A pretty, lithe boy stood smiling on the threshold with a summons from Fionn. Tuiren must rush to the dun to make a feast for her nephew's guests and among them was Muirne. Tuiren wrapped herself against the chill and went out.

Thus she followed the boy along the path, and when they had gone awhile, Uchtdealb pulled a hazel rod from her cloak and struck Tuiren a hard blow and chanted

Fith-fath will I make on thee
By Brigit of the bubbling spring
By the milk of the moon
By Morrigna of the augury
From woman to bitch

From wife to hound
From mother to bearer of dogs. . . .

And Tuiren changed into the loveliest, most graceful, glorious russet hound that ever was seen.

And she sat on her haunches on the clothing that had dropped from her human body and scratched her ear and licked her chops. She padded obediently awhile behind Uchtdealb, sniffing the air and weedy earth, delighted by her hound shape and by the fresh simplicity that calmed her heart.

And Uchtdealb led Tuiren along the coast by the crashing sea. Tuiren yipped at the bright, stark moon. She chased the glistening foam on the waves as it streaked across the horizon and she breathed the salty air. Despite Uchtdealb's impatient commands, Tuiren dug furiously in the sand, bounced after skittering crabs, splashed in pools, drew circles on the shore with her rump and sampled sweet carrion all along the way.

Thus they progressed until at last they reached the house of Fergus Fionnliath, the king of the harbor of Gallimh.

Now it happened that Fergus despised dogs. He hated hounds so much he would not allow them in his house, for the dog was guardian of death and scavenged the flesh of the departed. And Fergus loved life such that death was to him intolerable, such that he would not honor the divinities of death, and so he half lived.

Thus he was shocked when Uchtdealb, glamoured as the

boy messenger, said she had been sent by Fionn to ask that Fergus care for the Rigfennid's favorite hound until he came to fetch her.

And Uchtdealb warned Fergus to take special care and mind the hound well, for this was the finest hunting dog in the world, the bravest, most loyal and clever hound on Earth, and she was with young.

And the faerie departed, much satisfied with herself, while Fergus wondered why Fionn mac Cumhall would send him a dog. Yet Fergus could refuse Fionn nothing; but he avoided the creature like a sickness.

Now, for the first time, Tuiren set out to charm a man. Whenever Fergus took up his spear and dagger, Tuiren trotted to his side and grinned and wagged her tail and her merry eyes sparkled and her happiness was nearly irresistible. Still Fergus looked on her with suspicion.

And it happened that one day, as he reached for his dagger, unnerved by the constant presence of the dog, he cut his finger on the blade. The blood flushed forth, and as Fergus stared at the wound, Tuiren licked her long tongue over it and, though Fergus jumped away, the dog's spittle stopped the bleeding and the wound healed then and there.

Now Fergus softened. He gave in to Tuiren's canine flirtations and finally he took her on the hunt. And the skill with which Tuiren stalked the game and brought it down soon turned Fergus's heart altogether. He came to love the copper hound and call her his beauty and his darling and brag of her to any who would listen.

And at evening, by the hearth, Fergus Fionnliath scratched Tuiren's ears. He stroked her red fur. He rested his feet on her back. She slept at the foot of his bed, and when morning came, the two, the former hater of hounds and the former homely woman, left the house together and never did they return empty-handed. And the dog Fergus believed signaled death brought him to life and defended him against strangers and attended his affections and was an unerring friend and gave him happiness.

Now Tuiren's teats dragged the ground. She felt her birth pangs. She sought a quiet place to hide. Fergus hurried to make her comfortable, bidding straw and blankets be laid beneath the laboring hound, admonishing his wives and servants to look after her. Then Fergus retreated and paced the harbor to and fro.

Now Iollan, for fear of Fionn, had never told the Rigfennid of Tuiren's disappearance. But sly verse and gossip among the talkative Fianna at last brought word to Fionn that his aunt was with child, but that she no longer lived at Iollan's house.

And Fionn arrived at Iollan's house with a retinue of Fianna, with Caoilte and Goll and Lugaidh Lamha, his closest companions. He demanded the whereabouts of his aunt. But Iollan could not tell him, for he had not sought her.

And Fionn raged. He reminded Iollan of his sureties. He

threatened Iollan. The Fianna stepped forward to take revenge. Iollan cowered. He vowed that if he did not find Tuiren in three days, he would give himself up for satisfaction and they could take his head and display it on a pole at the great gate of the dun.

Thus the Rigfennid departed Iollan's house. As soon as Fionn was out of sight, Iollan dashed to the river, to the rock hidden by the rose briar, and there he whistled once, twice, three times for Uchtdealb, who appeared out of the thorns in a blaze of indignant golden hair.

Now she was covered in a garment of mourning linen, fists planted on her hips, eyebrows raised in challenge. Iollan reached for her, but she stepped away. He confessed his pledge to Fionn. And Uchtdealb mocked Iollan and smirked, and when he was done pleading and begging forgiveness, she tossed her hair and teased him with one fair breast. And then she made him swear that if she returned Tuiren to Fionn, Iollan would be her sweetheart forever.

And Iollan stepped through the door that separates this world from the Other. By the time the rose-briar curtain tangled behind him, Uchtdealb had already arrived at the harbor of Gallimh at the house of Fergus Fionnliath. Again she was disguised as the messenger boy, now come to claim Fionn mac Cumhall's favorite hound and whatever litter she had.

And Fergus greeted her glumly, while Tuiren snapped her teeth and snarled at Uchtdealb.

Now Fergus the Hater of Hounds wept bitterly as the copper dog left his house. And Tuiren whimpered and whined and barked against leaving, but Uchtdealb carried her two white pups, whelps with bright red ears. Tuiren followed. But she turned her head back and back and back again to look at Fergus as she limped away, tail tucked between her legs.

Now Uchtdealb of the Fair Breast produced her hazel rod and struck the hound and chanted:

Fith-fath will I make on thee
By Brigit of the bubbling spring
By the milk of the moon
By Morrigna of the augury
From bitch to woman
No more a hound.
But in human form
Iollan's pups will never be. . . .

And Tuiren was rendered back into a woman, as homely as ever. The faerie threw her cape at Tuiren, then handed her the two white whelps with bright red ears and disappeared.

And reappeared behind the rose-briar curtain, where Iollan waited, trapped within the Sidhe.

Now Tuiren walked downcast along the shore and into the woods and to the dun marked by the oak. And she knocked on Fionn's great gate, clutching her litter. Fionn greeted Tuiren with exultation and the Fianna gathered round to welcome her. But all the druidry on Earth could not change the two white pups into human babes, for the jealous fith-fath had been set firmly upon them.

Thus Fionn claimed them and named his hound cousins Bran and Sceolan and they were ever his dearest friends in this or any other world. And their natures were nearly as human as Fionn's was nearly beast.

And Tuiren agreed to marry Lugaidh Lamha, who asked for her, for Fionn had given her the property Iollan left behind. And Muirne attended the wedding feast and each man there yearned for her attentions—each, that is, except Fergus Fionnliath, who hung behind and had no appetite for celebrating.

Now Tuiren the Homely was called Tuiren the Dog. No longer would they let her race or hunt or play the Fianna's sports with them. For safety's sake, they said, that she not be moonstruck by any remains of Uchtdealb's fith-fath, and thus give birth again to hounds.

Thus Tuiren stayed home and had many more young, all of them human and some of them homely. And though she was confined and dreamed each day of that brief happiness with Fergus, she learned to take pleasure in Lugaidh's bed, for then she imagined herself once again in the shape of a beautiful russet hound, and this Lugaidh never knew.

And it came to pass, after restless years, when the moon was full and milky, Tuiren could bear her confines no longer. She stole from her house and her housewifely duties. And hidden alone by a bubbling spring, she made the fith-fath, for she had ever preserved Uchtdealb's words in her memory, just as all the Fianna could remember poetry quick as it met their hearing.

Fith-fath will I make on me . . .

she chanted, and dropped to her knees and her long nose and chin met in an elegant pointed muzzle and her ears grew floppy and her feet and hands turned to padded paws and she sat on her haunches and scratched her belly and then did the merriment return to her eyes and the wet grin return to her mouth.

Now she raced to the harbor house of Fergus Fionnliath, chasing gray waves and bellowing at the green sky.

And when Fergus answered her high bark at his door, he sobbed for joy and bent to embrace her and she slapped her paws on his shoulders and licked the tears from his face and wagged her tail and bayed. She spent the night at the foot of his bed and at dawn they rose together and set out on the hunt.

And each full moon she made the fith-fath and returned to Fergus Fionnliath, who kept Tuiren the Hound's secret always.

II
The Doe

You rise before the sun. Alert to the uproar of hounds. You travel the path of the setting moon. You stalk the hunters.

You sense them, then you see them. No hair on their heads skims branches or leaves as they dip through the woodland. No twigs crunch underfoot. Hounds' snouts trace your scent along the ground. Men and dogs listen left and right and watch the brush for tiny signs.

You shift in the dappled forest light, drawing their attention. You start and the hounds rise up baying. Bellowing shakes the air. The Fianna burst after the dogs. You spring over rocks and streams.

You run and run. The hunters drop back one by one and their dogs retreat. One man stays the chase. His two white hounds pant after you and he laughs with the effort. Is he, at last, the one you've sought?

This is how you'll be sure:

You rush out of the dark, protective wood, leading hounds

and hunter into a sunny, open valley. The dogs have room to kill. The hunter's blade can clearly find its mark. You lie down on green grass. The hounds plunge. The hunter grips his silver dagger. The hounds fall on you. They lick your neck and nuzzle your nose. They wag their tails and grin and whine with joy. The hunter looks on in wonder.

Fionn mac Cumhall whistles and they obey. He walks swiftly back to his dun. You follow. Step for step, while the hounds he calls Bran and Sceolan frolic around his feet and yours. You follow them past the oak that marks the dun, straight past the great gate and into the hall.

The Fianna exclaim and tease at the sight of Fionn and his hounds pursued by a doe. The Rigfennid shrugs and sits to drink with them, while you creep into shadows. The flicker of antlers on the walls. Bone, shining transparent in torchlight. The Fianna forget you. They sing, recite and eat their fill. Fires are damped. The household retires.

Fionn dreams of deer. He dreams of pursuit and his legs flinch and twitch. You trace a small, thin finger lightly across his chest. He opens his eyes. He stares at your face, but he averts his gaze from your nakedness. He is unable to shake himself from the bewildering dream that seems to have transformed a hind into a woman at his bedside. You stand over him. Your voice is weak. You are unused to speaking.

This is what you tell him:

My name is Sadb and I am the doe you hunted this day. I was put in that shape for refusing the love of Fear Doirche, the druid of Dea. For three years I have lived the life of a deer in the far part of Ireland. Trapped. More afraid of the druid than of huntsmen. If I relented and let Fear Doirche claim me, he would return my woman's shape. But I would not relent.

At last, his servant took pity on me. She had overheard Fear Doirche's fith-fath and she told me that if I could reach the dun of Fionn's Fianna, the druid would have no power over me, and that the red-eared hounds, Bran and Sceolan, whose nature is human like my own, would know me and defend me.

I stole from that territory and never stopped till now.

So strong is Fionn's love for you, he quits hunting and gives up all wild pleasures. When he must leave the dun, he leaves a guard for you and you wait for him by the gate, safe within, watching for his return with your bright brown eyes, tense and alert. When you hear the greeting barks of Bran and Sceolan, you start and run to Fionn and throw your arms around him. You frisk and play with his hound cousins.

One night, you are standing at the table behind the Rig-fennid. You serve his mead. You reach across him to pick food from his plate. You press your widening waist against his shoulders. He is sighing affections to you when men burst into the hall, crying news that the warriors of Lochlann have come against Ireland in ships so large whole forests were felled to build them.

Fionn stiffens. And you, having had no fear for nearly a year, jerk as if to bolt. But Fionn holds you still. He nods to his men. The Fianna rush here and there around the hall gathering weapons. Fionn tells you there is no choice but to go. The one-legged warriors of Lochlann are giants who eat raw human flesh, and fire, he says, shoots from the single eye sunk deep in their brows. It is a fire that scorches as far as that eye can see, and the eyes of the Lochlann warriors can see across mountains.

Fionn promises he will conquer them quickly and return to you soon. The Lochlann are big and terrifying, but they are no match for the Fianna. You smile. Your hands tremble.

You curl up by the gate. The indentation you leave in the grass is that of a deer in morning before breeze and day erase the evidence of its resting place. You don't rest. Your eyes are locked on the path beyond the gate. The guards mill about, playing chess, practicing arms, restless that they were not chosen to fight the Lochlann invaders.

The other women bring you food. They whisper that the Rigfennid's wife has not yet lost her animal ways. Some recall how you play with Bran and Sceolan as if they were kin. Your shyness. Your quick nerves. Your dreamy silence. The women agree you will befriend them and become more fully human when your child is born.

You simply watch the path. Aloof. Days crawl by. Two. Four. Five. You twist your gray-brown hair. You plait it and unplait it. You rub your belly in spirals to keep the infant warm and give it heat to help it grow. Till seven days seem like seven years.

The morning of the seventh day brings dreary skies and cold drizzle. The women plead with you to come inside. You ignore them, eyes fixed on the spectral outline of the oak that marks the dun.

Mist rolls thicker and thicker toward you, bringing with it the baying of Bran and the howling of Sceolan and the sweet call of Fionn's hunting horn.

The women and guards try to hold you, but you pull away. You dash from the safety of the dun with outstretched arms. The arms stretched out to you that catch you are not warm Fionn's but the thin, white-hard limbs of Fear Doirche.

Though he is glamoured in the likeness of Fionn, you know him instantly. You scream and struggle. You twist this way and that in his grasp, but the druid strikes you with his hazel rod.

Fith-fath will I make on thee
By the sun disk of Lugh
By the golden goblet of Eriu
By Morrigna of the augury
From woman to hind
From maiden to doe
From girl to deer. . . .

Gray-brown fur quickens all across your flesh. Your nose and forehead lengthen. Your hands and feet shrink and harden into hooves. You turn three times and gallop toward the gate, but the raging hounds disguised as Bran and Sceolan bite your throat and clamp your thigh and drag you away and herd you into the blind mist.

The guards stumble high and low through the fog following

every murmur. The women shout and wail for you. But you have vanished.

At dusk, the rain has dried. Fionn hurries home, thinking how you'll look and feel, thinking of your happy noise when you spy him coming through the gate and how you'll greet him. But as soon as they pass the oak that marks the dun, Bran and Sceolan slide to their bellies and slither and moan. There is no sign of you. No one waits and watches. The returning Fianna look in desperation on the emptiness and on Fionn's despair. The fith-fath of Fear Doirche echoes faintly in the growing night. Fionn sinks to the ground where you sat and winds the flattened grass around his fingers. He stares at your deer's contour as if he could conjure you. He strikes his breast and loosens tears. He rises heavily and staggers to the bed you shared. He lies there day and night for three nights and three days with his back to the others.

Then he heaves himself from his stupor, and through the length of seven years, he seeks you in every far corner of Ireland. He touches no other woman. He hunts only with his five most trustworthy hounds and lets them be led by Bran and Sceolan so that there will be no danger to you if he ever comes on your track.

One day, when your child is strong enough, when he has developed his own odor and mettle, you hear the familiar barking and baying of hounds and hunting horns. You let the boy go to Bran and Sceolan.

III
The Fawn

Niamh waits at Tir na n'Og. Twenty years in the human world is half an hour in the Other. A century passes in a night of lovemaking.

Niamh's wait is long and brief. Sure enough, the white steed materializes. The horse on which her man, Oisin, left her, its saddle girth loose and swaying. The horse nudges her arm. She embraces its neck.

She consults no one. She offers no farewells. She buckles the saddle. She swings onto it. She turns the horse back the way it came.

A doe watches as Niamh rides from the Country of the Young, lightly gripping her ringing bridle, cloudless eyes fixed straight ahead, riding up from the place where she was born when time began, the country she has left only once before, when she fetched Oisin to love her.

The doe follows Niamh past the emerald sea through blue and silver mists. Over meadows that bloom without end, along a path of crystal cobbles lined with velvet ferns and trees drooping with abundance. A willow catches Niamh's hair and tugs as if to hold her in the safety of the Sidhe.

This is not the route Oisin took out of Tir na n'Og. In that moment, the white steed splashed through the foam and flew up and over the faerie palaces with their bright sun bowers and lime-white walls that dance on the surface of the sea. Niamh, whose heart is unhindered by time, travels gradually.

The path rises. The doe bounds along the steep slope. She stops at the frontier between the worlds, where the eternal balm of Tir na n'Og turns to earthly winter and frost bends the trees. Her eyes fill with sorrow and envy, but she will go no farther.

Niamh crosses the border and wraps her silken mantle close about her shoulders. She knows nothing of seasons. She wonders how Oisin fares in this cold world. An unsettled man. Dispassionate, until the songs glimmer from his harp. He is fleet and shy and gentle and homesick.

Dry leaves crunch on heaved, hard ground beneath the white steed's shoes. A magpie screams and snow falls. It is easy to be invisible in this harsh gloom. Why did Oisin mac Fionn return to this vale of death and decay despite Niamh's warning?

An old, old man sits in a monastery cell. Wind cruises through cracks in stone walls. He is blind and his joints creak when he shifts on the hard bench where he has been sitting since the people brought him here when he fell from the white steed.

His faerie garments, torc of gold, silver cloak of satin and red-gold leather armor, drape like dead skin on his emaciated body. His toes clench his oversized boots.

The old man's clothing grows larger as his thoughts contract. He will enjoy this silence until Patrick returns with more entreaties to embrace a solitary god, a god all folk in Ireland now seem to follow, a possessive deity who broaches no companions, razes the forests and claims the sun and moon and will not feast with Fionn mac Cumhall and the men of the Fianna or honor them with riches.

Had not Patrick bade his scribes write the old man's songs of the heroes' deeds in this world and the Other? Does he not listen enrapt, begging like a child for more and more tales?

Why, then, has the monk not understood that the Fianna, free men of the wild, who refused no one in need, sought always to destroy tyrants and invaders?

"Truth was in our hearts, and strength in our arms and fulfillment in our tongues," the old man tells Patrick.

"A god who would confine generous Fionn to suffering in a pit of fire because Fionn had never known or heard of him?" The old man is astonished. "Were your god in bonds, Fionn would fight to free him. Fionn left none in pain or danger."

The old man drifts. Roman Patrick's arguments cannot restrain the flood of nostalgia and regret for another world, stories that are his own, with which he will not entertain the monk. The picture of a mute, naked boy takes shape behind his eyes:

The boy played beside a stream while his mother drank. Baying and barking and shouting closed all around. His mother bolted into the bushes. The boy shinnied up a tree. From his high perch, he searched for her, afraid to find her torn to pieces by hunting dogs. But she was gone and the dogs whined and scratched the tree trunk.

A man called and coaxed. At last, the boy, sensing no harm, lowered himself branch by branch and landed in the man's arms. He looked the boy full in the face. He stroked the fur that grew from the boy's eyebrow along his temple, brown fur dotted with white. He wept.

The boy marveled. This was the second man he had ever seen. But while this one was small and stocky, muscular, tan and warm, the first had been beardless, thin, and blue as skimmed milk. He had visited the boy's mother many times in the cave where they had taken shelter. He had spoken to her in wheedling, cajoling tones. She had cringed from him until he departed in anger, leaving a menacing aura.

This man, Fionn mac Cumhall, held the boy in a solid, happy embrace. "Little Fawn, my son. You've come home," he laughed. "Seven years I've searched for you and your mother," he said. He stood abruptly, looked about, beat the bushes halfheartedly like one who had worn a long, tired habit to the nub. He called "Sadb! Sadb!" but there was no sign of life and Fionn mac Cumhall again hugged the bewildered boy and sighed.

Then the boy was wrestling on the ground with Bran and Sceolan, who slavered and nipped him while he pulled their red ears as if they were old friends.

Now he is merely old. This groaning age has come upon him so terribly and suddenly.

The cell door opens and the monk enters bearing a bowl of broth. Fasting and prayer and flagellation. There is no laughter, no hardiness in this new world, where Patrick's god is cramped within church walls.

The monk hands the bowl to the old man. He mutters thanks and takes it with trembling hands. His white beard drags in the gruel. Patrick of Rome picks it out and sits beside him and begins again his pious persuasions. The old, old man, who is blind and shrinking, wishes he were also deaf.

The doe grazes in a glade just at the edge of the human world. A trail of red stars still hangs where the faerie Niamh passed out of Tir na n'Og. The doe looks wishfully at the scarlet shimmer. She would also go into the human world but for dangers whose details she now only barely recalls.

Her mind's pictures swirl around a relentless white light in the form of a long, thin man. The cold figure has always lurked there.

He captured her and she escaped and he captured her again. Round and round him she ran. With every step, she changed from hind to woman or woman to hind.

There is another man, and he, too, pursues her. He is warm and tan and sturdy and safe. Sometimes, he leaps into the doe's memory followed by two white hounds. Sometimes, he is in the mirthful company of other men.

Secure in his dun, the doe was transformed into woman and wife. Then she had a name and she lived happily awhile. But the beardless man, who burned determined as noon, found her, tricked her, trapped her, and with the fith-fath he recast her and led her away.

Fionn mac Cumhall struck his fist against his chest. He searched glen and ravine, mountain and wood, coast and cavern, calling "Sadb! Sadb!" She could not penetrate the thin, hard light to reach him.

Blood and water on a cave floor. A human infant sliding from between the twitching thighs of a deer.

The ever-present, beardless man watched from shadow as the doe licked the baby's temple. A patch of brown fur flecked with white sprouted where her thick, coarse tongue licked and cleaned the membrane from the little boy's head.

The fearful yelping of hounds. The shouts of hunters. The boy scrambling up a tree. The doe rushing frantically into the hard light of the beardless man. His hazel wand whistling around her. His fith-fath made her invisible to Fionn mac Cumhall.

"Have I lived so long that Fionn and the Fianna are worm-eaten in their graves?" the old man mutters. "Where are they?"

He has traveled so far through time and found no one and nothing but a pitiful, woodless place, where once strong men are now rooted to husbandry, dwarfed in the confines of fortresses, humbled by a disdainful god. At the cooking places of the Fianna, there is desiccated silence. The great oak that marked the dun is gone. A rubble of weeds and nettle and moss-covered stones where Fionn's great hall stood.

Roman Patrick's tonsure gleams in the cell's wretched light. "The limbs of the mighty Fianna are torn and scorched on the burning slabs of hell."

The old man reaches for the patch on his temple. Age has left bare and tented skin. Never has shame been put on him till now. "If the brown leaves were gold that the wood lets fall, if the white waves were silver, Fionn would have given it all away."

The monk sighs. "Your false deities are dead, conquered by the one true god. The paradise of which you sing is wicked and profane."

"And the hounds?" the old man mumbles. "Will Bran and Sceolan greet me in heaven with their happy yells?"

"Animals have no souls," Patrick replies, and he leans into the old man's face, hot breath fluttering the white beard, as if to demonstrate the devil's heat.

What are flimsy, pale angels to the Fianna? They would overcome Patrick's devil as if he were a weak infant. The old man opens his mouth to speak, then hardens into silence. A young swordsman appears in the old man's mind, a youth who had been mute, but when he finally learned human speech it was poetry and he sang with his harp by the fires of the Fianna. Patrick rumbles on, punctuating his sermon with demands for more tales about Fionn and Fianna. But the old man is lost again in the mist that drizzled on the youth one morning long ago.

Hunt-wandering overcame him as day suddenly turned to night. He was separated from his dogs and his companions and he meandered alone and weary. He stumbled into a luminous valley, where a doe grazed placidly.

She turned to him with yearning eyes. "Follow me, fawn of my heart."

He stared at the creature, fearful he might burst with love.

They came to a rock in the base of a hill. She lifted a leaf with her mouth and the rock opened. They entered a bright cavern, lit gold with many tallows. Tapestries covered rough walls, and brocade covered soft seats. Inside, the doe became a woman.

"I am your mother from whom you were parted long ago," she said. "You are hungry and tired. Come, Oisin, Little Fawn, sit down and rest."

She placed food and drink before him, and when he had done feasting, she gave him a harp and he sang the stories of Fionn mac Cumhall. The woman who was his mother and a doe sobbed quietly.

The old man snores, dreaming of the young man asleep on his mother's lap while she sang to him.

My darling, my dun buck,
My spirit and my delight.
Fairim, firim, obh, obh.
May I not hear of your wounding,
may I not see you weep.
My calf, my foal, my fair one.

For three days the youth slept, and when he woke, he said, "I must go, Mother, to the Fianna."

She kissed his cheek three times. She touched the tip of her tongue to his salty temple. She opened the door in the rock, and under the evening sky, she changed from woman to hind.

When he found his company, it was not three days but three years that had passed.

The old man wakes with a start. "How long, Patrick, since I last walked this land in the footsteps of the Fianna?"

"Half a thousand years, but time is short. Repent and be saved. You will have eternal life."

"Monk, I had eternal life. It was mine in the lap of my mother and mine at Tir na n'Og in the arms of Niamh. Yet I chose to return, to visit mortal seasons with Fionn and my brothers. Whether they now reside in your heaven or in your hell, there I will go with them."

A supple young voice resounds in the doe's memory even as she rests secure now in the balm of Tir na n'Og. The song of her son which never fades. The song of caution he daily chanted into the forests and hills and plains after he had left her golden cavern.

If you are my mother and you a deer,
arise before the sunrise.
If you are my mother and you a deer,
beware the blade in every hunter's hand,
beware the hounds of uproar, hounds of rage
in battle-fury before you.

Niamh's journey continues. Her eyes dart across the dark terrain seeking clues. The beauty with which she can overpower all men illuminates the land. That beauty with which she transfixed Fionn and the Fianna on the day she claimed Oisin.

She rode the white steed dressed in queen's raiment. Her summoning song as she entered Fionn's camp cast a drowsy stillness over the trees, the sky, the birds, the hounds and the men.

The song ended and Fionn recovered his own voice. "Where do you come from, maiden, and what do you want from me?"

The daughter of the King of the Land of Youth announced her intention.

"Of all men," Fionn asked, "why Oisin?"

She did not answer, but looked from the Rigfennid to his son. She had spied on Oisin as he wandered through woods and fields, remote in the rowdy fellowship of the Fianna, strong and graceful yet skittish, eyes distant as if he were seeking something lost lifetimes ago. She had disguised herself as a fly on his chessboard. As sheen on the strings of his harp, as red stars circling his campfires. She had hidden in the dark of the moon and listened to his songs. She watched him until she was distraught with love and desire.

"Will you go with me, Oisin, to my father's land, to Tir na n'Og?"

She sat her horse before him, so radiant he lost all resolve and forgot his love for all things but her. "I will go with you to the world's end," he said.

He kissed his father. Fionn ran his fingers through the fur on Oisin's temple. "I have no hope that you'll come back to me, Little Fawn," he said.

Oisin mounted the white steed behind Niamh and they departed against the stream of Fionn mac Cumhall's lament.

Niamh still feels Oisin's arms around her waist exactly as they were that day. Once again, she sings her summoning song that Oisin might reveal his whereabouts.

An endless feast, unceasing music
in the land beyond all dreams.
Come, Oisin, to wild honey
and wine that never fails.

Come to fruit and flower.
You will have horses
and hounds that outrun the wind.
A magic blade
and Niamh to love you all your days.

The memories spur her impatience. Niamh shakes the horse's ringing bridle. "My beauty, my dancer. Quickly. Can you find the place where you left him?

The white steed shoots like a sunbeam across the plain. Soon they stand at the mouth of a quarry, where small, feeble men gasp and grunt, hauling granite and marble.

The land is dotted with tiny stick-and-mud huts. The faerie Niamh thinks how cruel and foolish Oisin was to leave her. For a time in Tir na n'Og he was content. But the Country of the Young was too tame, too pretty. Ecstasy turned to evasion. Restlessness for the mortal world. To roam and hunt and fight with the Fianna. Back and forth, from faerie to human, Oisin migrated his whole life long. And thinking of his wandering, Niamh feels very old. She is forever sheltered, forever fixed in maidenhood. But what if her feet were now to touch the ground? Would she dissolve into dust?

She seeks Oisin—to plead for his return or mourn his death—but she has no notion of human years, nor how many have gone since Oisin went away with her. Yet staring into the quarry, she sees that in whatever time that was, free men have

150

become enslaved, and the wilderness, once so like the balmy green of Tir na n'Og, has disappeared. In the quarry below, puny, straining men, sweating despite the winter cold, pound rocks for taskmasters.

She sits on the white steed watching until one man's eye catches hers. She calls so none but he can hear. He raises his arm to his forehead to shield himself against her brilliance. She exhales and with her breath suspends the others in their gestures. She inhales and draws the quarryman up the sides of the black pit. He shifts from foot to foot before her, eyes downcast, quivering and terrified.

At last, he stammers, "Great shining queen, are you an angel who rides the devil's stallion?"

Who or what are devils and angels? Niamh wonders. Aloud she says simply, "Tell me."

"A warrior fell from this horse not five days ago," the man answers.

"How did he fall?" Her voice is so sweet it emboldens him.

"Men were trapped under a marble slab. Dying. We could not move it. The slab would not budge.

"Just then, a warrior pranced toward us. On that very horse. In foreign dress. He was tall and mighty, with sword-blue eyes and ruddy cheeks. His teeth were like pearls and his yellow curls clustered beneath his helmet like a halo. We thought he, too, must be an angel come to free us from toil and care. A messenger from heaven, come to save the souls of the men crushed beneath the rock.

"Then we saw that one eyebrow spread full across his temple in fur with the markings of a fawn, and some among us were afraid."

Niamh smiles and nods encouragement. The man grows confident.

"The warrior leaned from the saddle, and with a huge, one-handed heave, he lifted the marble slab. But as he leaned into the stone, and as it rolled back down the pit, his saddle girth unbuckled and he slipped headlong off the horse and landed on the ground.

"In that instant, this horse vanished. It *was* this steed and this same saddle, too. The withered thing that rose from the ground teetering was no youthful warrior but an old, old man."

"And then?"

"We fled. Then we knew the fur on his temple was the mark of the devil. We ran as he moaned and groped blindly at the air and fell again and again."

"You deserted him? Alone and sightless? He who had rescued you? Men have become cowards."

The quarryman loses the rhythm of his story. He cringes when Niamh raises the flat of her hand above his head. "Go on!" she orders.

"Great queen. Blessed angel. Please. We turned back when we saw that the doom had been wrought for him alone. Then we lifted him up and asked him who he was.

"My lady, sure he was daft. He claimed to be son of Fionn mac Cumhall, gone half a thousand years. We took him to Patrick. It is five days. Sure by now he is dead and absolved. Since holy Patrick came to Ireland with psalms and prayers to cleanse us from sin and save us from . . ."

But Niamh has left the man to finish telling his tale to a wreath of red stars, while the others within the quarry, released from the spell, laugh at him as if he were talking to fireflies.

Patrick dismisses his scribes. The old, old man is dying and will no longer speak. The monk has rid the land of druids and oaks and built his seven hundred churches in every corner. For five days, he has savored Oisin's tales of the Fianna, story after story of love and war that enchant the monk, and he craves the old man's voice. In his sleep, Patrick mutters a fith-fath, and in his dreams, his body shifts to that of a handsome roebuck. Every morning, he prays for absolution and scourges himself on his god's behalf.

What life is left to Oisin has been kept pulsing by Patrick's demands for songs. The tales have turned to rattles in his throat. He sees his mother in her golden cavern. He hears the high blasts of hunting horns and the joyful barks of Bran and Sceolan. There is no pleasure without Fionn mac Cumhall and the Fianna.

The marble grandeurs of Roman Patrick's persistent heaven pale beside those of the green, gentle Land of Youth. The old man feels the fragile faerie bones of lovely Niamh pressing tight against him, while century after century pass like minutes in Tir na n'Og.

And the deep dread that glazed Niamh's cloudless eyes as she spoke her warning:

If you must visit the human world,
if you must find your father,
I give you leave to go.
I give the white steed to carry you.

Swear, Oisin, swear,
promise that your feet
will never touch the ground.

He had found the hunting places of the Fianna, he had found the site of Fionn's great dun—all destroyed by time. And he had meant to return to Tir na n'Og, but he had fallen from the white steed and helpless age had overtaken him.

Patrick follows his scribes out the cell door. He will bring holy water for last rites. For his own soul's sake and in gratitude for the old man's songs, the monk will assure his passage into heaven and pray each day for the soul of Oisin mac Fionn despite his protestations.

Patrick is not present when red stars sift through the cracks in the monastery wall. They twirl about the cell and embrace the wizened figure barely alive on the hard bench.

When the monk returns, the cell is empty. The old, old man is gone.

In Tir na n'Og she is free. The doe cannot recall how she got here or why Fionn mac Cumhall no longer seeks her or why the cold, beardless man no longer visits her except in memory. She is free from all but loneliness.

The fog at the frontier between the human and faerie realms is lifting. The doe's keen ears perceive the beat of hooves. She steps quickly, lightly behind a tree. There are no hunting horns, no hounds baying.

FITH-FATH SUITE

Shadows turn to silhouettes in the gloaming. Galloping straight toward her. The faerie Niamh appears bent low on her white steed. Red stars describe a trail behind her and tangle in the horse's mane.

Come, Oisin, to wild honey,
to wine that never fails.
Come to fruit and flower....

Niamh laughs and sings. A little fawn, antlers budding, races alongside her, and together they burst across the border between the worlds.

The doe emerges cautiously from her hiding place. The fawn tilts his head and nudges her belly. She passes her strong, coarse tongue over his white-speckled temple.

Niamh veers toward the emerald sea. Still laughing, she disappears into silver froth. She will meet Oisin again. When spring is on the Earth, his stag's bell will call her up.

Retold from versions by Michael Comyn, Padraic Colum, Lady Augusta Gregory, and W. B. Yeats, and in *The Carmina Gaedelica*. With thanks to John Wright.

THE ROMANCE OF MIS AND DUBH RUIS

A *caoineadh* is a long, extempore poem of eulogy and lament, sung at wakes and funerals, usually by women in honor of men. Much of the greatest Irish poetry has been created by "wailing women." Singing the *caoineadh* is a rite of separation, whereby the mourner briefly joins the departed in the limnal space between life and death and by the act of keening and versifying can let go the grief and return to daily life.

Mis stumbled onto the battlefield. Rifled through tranquil death. Even the ravens were mute.

Daire Mor's head and golden torc had been taken for trophy. She knew him by his knuckles. By the scars on knuckles that had tickled her ears when she sat beside him on the king's seat in the banquet hall. When he rode her proudly on his back through the clans. When he drove her into the villages on his chariot adorned with beaten gold. At night, he covered her with calfskins, and beamed at her in her bedbox while her mother sang. When Mis's mother died, Daire Mor wept openly and wailed *caoineadh* like a woman.

The residue of his wide smile was a notched scarlet slash on his empty shoulders where a curved ax had fallen. Mis caught his streaming blood in cupped palms and drank. Sucked his wounds. Licked his bruises. She curled into his shrinking ribs and laid her head on his chest.

She wallowed in shriveling tissue and sinew. Hummed her mother's lullaby. But her voice could compose no lamenting verse to honor him. She could not keen, she could not sing *caoineadh*.

Daire Mor's body stiffened. Then softened. Carrion birds ignored Mis. Unfastened Daire Mor's skin. Squabbled for

ON THE EDGE OF DREAM

morsels. Each organ was a gem. The ruby heart. The sapphire lung. The garnet liver. The diamond spleen.

Rain. Sleet. Heat. Mis lay close against the puckering meat. Stink penetrated her nostrils. Melted the last of her reason. Dogs came. Snarled for scraps. Tore bones from joints. Scattered spine and hip. Mis stretched her tongue to her father and scooped black soil.

She stood. Lurched and limped. She could not remember where she was or why. Her pretty leather boots and bright frock were rags. Golden brooch stolen by magpies. Hair clotted with blood and guts, marrow and excrement, moss and dirt.

She walked. The only child of a raiding chieftain lost in strange terrain and brain-sick. Her unguided path veered upward. Toward a mountain. To a cave. She hid in the suffocating dark.

She forgot her father. Blackened the last picture of him from her mind. Her people, her home, her language, all love regressed to nothing. Speechless, thoughtless, without memory.

Hair sprouted over Mis's body until it swept her heels. Raging appetite pulled at her skinny belly. She scented and stalked beast, bird and man. She rushed swift as wind. Wind outstripped nameless wrath. Outraced pain. Mis caught every beast, every bird, every man who ventured onto her mountain. Her long nails toughened into talons. She ripped and shredded. Killing gave form to her grief and fury. She filled her cupped palms with blood. Filled her belly with gore. Bones piled high on Mis's mountain.

Game grew scarce. The mountain a wilderness. Now and then a cow or sheep wandered from the herd. The shepherd followed. Their bones increased Mis's trophies.

She stared at the sky. Sniffed at the dirt. Licked it. Picked at fleas and lice. Huddled in her cave, she slept. She never dreamed. But the scent of death danced through her sleep.

They named that deserted country Clanmaurice. And the King of Munster issued a proclamation that Mis should not be killed, for he was curious to see the wild maiden who ravished all life that came near her like an unshriven ghost. He promised a great reward together with the settlement and rent of Clanmaurice to whoever could bring her into custody alive. And many worthy warriors tried, but Mis devoured them all.

Madness pounded Mis's hearing. Banged like warclappers. Through that relentless din, one day, Mis heard a song.

Long, deep tones shimmered up her mountain. Long and smooth. Not busy birdsong, or any tune Mis had ever known. Cadence that penetrated the cacophony. Melody borne by breezes, reflected on trickling water. Woven round with a human voice, like strong, spiraling silver.

She struggled to listen. To block the ever-present clang of spears and trumpets, screams and swords. To capture the pure nimble notes skittering toward her. The song reeled. She grabbed for it. It ambushed her from behind. She swatted at it. The music fled. Resonated with shifting leaves. Swooped. Encased her. Scratched at Mis's heart.

A high tremor. She crept toward the source. The note dipped. One strain forged into another. Music shook the desolation of Mis's mountain. She hid behind a tree. In the distance she saw a young man sitting cross-legged playing a harp. Plump, inquisitive lips puckered in song.

Dubh Ruis, the king's harper, took up the king's challenge. He asked for gold and gold was granted, for gold was a part of the harper's plan to rescue the wild maiden of Clanmaurice.

Mis growled. She leaped down the mountain. Three leaps

and hair like wings. Claws flashing. Shrieking. She burst at the trespasser.

He did not move. Did not look up. Dainty knuckles. Eloquent fingers. He stroked his harp with a loving, soothing hand.

She circled to plunge at him. A brilliant, wriggling glint caught her eye. She halted. The stranger's cloak lay glimmering before him on the ground. Mis tried to yowl. The screech stuck in her throat. She stared at the golden gleam. Yellow nuggets arranged on blue silk. She tipped her head. Crouched and reached for the glittering pebbles. Wavering. Hesitant. It was gold the color of her father's beard and of his regal torc. Gold like his polished chariot. Like the blazing hearth in the banquet hall. Like her mother's rings and bracelets. Like her own golden brooch.

Flickers of home and clan. The brief, muffled recollection jolted Mis from her void, but quick as they came, the memories retreated.

Dubh Ruis played on. Mis wobbled with curiosity. Touched the precious stuff. Recoiled. Glanced at the harper, who ignored her and played on and on. She touched the gold again and whimpered. He plucked a note. The same hypnotic note. He smiled at Mis. Shy, beardless, fearless, girlish smile. She glowered at him through curtains of filthy hair.

The note droned. He reached for her. Set his free hand on her knee. She flinched. Backed away on her heels. He inched closer. His hand slid up her thigh. She would not take her sight from the golden nuggets. The glitter held her while his agile fingers outlined the shape of her strong leg beneath its pelt. She squatted. Waited. Tense. Suspicious. The gold sparkled in sunshine.

Dubh Ruis set down his harp. He parted the heavy wall of Mis's hair. Hair on her chest. Fur cascading along her stomach, laid flat in swirls on her buttocks. Mis guarded the nuggets with her eyes while his fingers sought the virginal delta between her legs. He traced bristling crevices. He found the dry, tight center, mired in anger and puerility, closed and unfledged. The untutored button.

She closed her eyes. Raised her hips. Weird yearning vibrated lower and lower while he chanted. He rubbed and caressed. Sweat and quim flooded the mane on her limbs.

She murmured and sighed. His fingers twisted gently round and round. Fiddling and strumming. In and out. In and out. *Be calm, be still, my girl, my darling, my daughter, my sister, my friend.* He stroked harder and faster. In and out. Her eyes rolled back. She moaned and trembled. And the estranged body, hardened by hatred, came to rest, soft as a pond.

Dubh Ruis put his fingers in her mouth. Mis tasted strange, fragrant fluids, the venerable nectar of women.

Mis lay drowsy. Dubh Ruis's skin was fair and pink, his curls tight and winsome. His scent was sweet and stout. Unthreatening. He grinned. Petted the bald soles of her feet with her own hair. Tickling brought forth the picture of Daire Mor. She tried to shove it away. But his name spun in her head.

When the beat of her father's name had ended, when her body stopped pulsating and she could breathe again, Mis jumped up. Dubh Ruis waited for deadly talons to take revenge. She rubbed her stomach. He nodded and chuckled. Rubbed his own stomach in agreement. She gestured frantically and leaped away. He turned his back. Stabbed his meat knife in the turf.

Mis leaped around her mountain. A stag appeared where no game had dared graze for years. She pursued it. Fleet and fatal. She caught it. Slashed its thigh. She dragged the crippled hart to the place where Dubh Ruis had dug a cooking pit. Where a cauldron of water boiled on the fire.

Proud of her catch, anxious to please, Mis clawed and lacerated the twitching deer. Dubh Ruis stepped between them. Gently pushed Mis aside. She snarled. He frowned. She cowered, afraid to displease him. He sliced the stag's throat. Meticulous. Singing a hymn of thanks to the stag. He skinned it. Butchered it. He dropped the meat into the boiling water.

The hirsute maiden and the beardless harper waited while the stew simmered, and its musty odor comforted Mis. Dubh Ruis sang songs of Mis's clan, of heroes' deeds, of Daire Mor and all her people's sires. She sat quietly beside him and played with the gold. And now and then, unaware of herself, she croaked along with him nonsensically: a snatch of lineage, a lyric nearly remembered.

Dubh Ruis made plates of hard, flat bread he took from his pouch. Served Mis the meal that she had caught and he had cooked. Mis clutched and gobbled. Dropped the meat. Dribbled and spit. Dubh Ruis fed her, until she could mimic his gestures. The way he held his breadplate firm and steady. Picked at the bloodless flesh with the fingers of his right hand. Folded the bread into a funnel to sip the juice. Wiped his mouth with the back of his hand. She stared at him, fascinated and blank.

When they were done, meat and breadplates consumed, Dubh Ruis took Mis's hand. Raised her from the ground. Guided her to the bubbling cauldron.

He lifted her into the water. Her heavy hair shielded her flesh against the boiling heat. Dubh Ruis saturated her feet and legs, her breasts and arms. Poured liquid over her head. Bathed her in the broth.

Glistening fat slid down Mis's fur. Pacified her itching skin.

He drizzled the cooking water on her head, her shoulders, her belly, again and again. He scooped the soup in his cupped palms, and Mis drank. Cordial odor. Soft and warm and easy to digest.

Strand by strand, bits of Mis's thatched hair shed as Dubh Ruis bathed and combed her.

The feral girl, the virginal daughter in the wilderness was fed boiled meat. Anointed with cooked food. And her rawness began to wash away.

Dubh Ruis prepared a bed. They lay together by the cooking pit. He cradled Mis. Rocked her the night long. She nestled into him like a cat. Snug as the calfskins with which her father had covered her. The texture of Dubh Ruis's tongue erased the awful taste of blood and dirt. They slept, but Mis did not dream.

Dubh Ruis stayed with Mis at the foot of her mountain across the summer months and she did not leap away. Though she had begun as a prize and a test Dubh Ruis had set to fathom the magic of music, now he loved her, as love comes from being needed, as mothers love their helpless newborns. He did not lure her to the king to exhibit her in shame, unformed, exposed. Day by day, he cared for her. Taught her to rest. To coax tunes from his harp. He carried her away from the terrifying war cries with lovely harmonies. He taught her to hunt with weapons. To ask permission of the game. To thank it once caught. The game increased in the increasing safety. Increased as if to offer itself to healing.

And Mis was calmed by his patience. Mesmerized by friendship she had not known since Daire Mor's death. Her voraciousness, the brutishness in which her infancy had been trapped, a beastliness that lacked the judiciousness of animals, gradually ebbed. Handful by handful each day, across that summer, the hair that smothered, concealed and swaddled Mis fell to the ground.

When bloodlust returned to overtake her, when Mis licked the dirt and menaced Dubh Ruis with snarls and claws, the harper gave her the gold nuggets to rub between her hands or suck between her teeth. By his lovemaking, her vigor transformed from loathing to affection. When at last Dubh Ruis cut Mis's talons with his meat knife and burned the cruel, ragged daggers in the campfire, Mis neither fought nor squirmed but acquiesced, trusting as a baby.

That night, Mis dreamed. She dreamed of Daire Mor. Restored and happy in death, her father embraced her. Kissed her cheek. Bid her farewell. In her dream, she saw again the terrible battlefield plush and green and blooming.

Mis woke keening. She wept and clapped and screamed. Her first clear spoken words a lament to honor Daire Mor. Verse after verse of the *caoineadh* she'd withheld so long stormed out of her mouth. She beat the ground. She bellowed and wailed. Bitter, tortured wailing that drove pain and anger into the ethos, into the arms of the merciful dead. The shriven dead who know the means to dispose of death.

With her *caoineadh*, the last of Mis's long, thick pelt disappeared. A handsome young woman with large, lively eyes emerged from the tangled, mossy mass.

Dubh Ruis consoled Mis while she spent the last of her sobs. He washed the tears from her cheeks. He brushed and plaited her smooth brown hair and dressed her in his cloak. Fastened it with a buckle he beat from the golden nuggets.

Dubh Ruis took Mis from the mountain, over the plain where battle had been done and autumn flowers now bloomed. He presented her to the King of Munster and Mis met the king proudly, eye to eye as the daughter of a chieftain come to take her own high seat.

The king gave Dubh Ruis the promised treasure together with the settlement and rent of Clanmaurice. But the harper's reward was greater still. He brought the savage maiden home, cured of her madness, expelled of childhood, released of the bond to her father, free from ghosts. Invested in womanhood, she grew wiser day by day and more accomplished year by year, and Dubh Ruis loved Mis as he loved the sun and the moon and music.

And Mis gave birth to four fine children and yearly honored her father's name. She stayed with Dubh Ruis forever until he died.

Then Mis called forth the other women. She removed her shoes and her jewels and loosened her hair. She dressed his body. She laid him out upon her table. She keened for him a caoineadh, verses beautiful and breathless. Music so magical it leaped three times from her mouth across the threshold between the living and the dead, and there contained and kept in readiness the story of their passion.

Retold from versions by Brian Ó'Cuív, Joseph Falaky Nagy and Angela Partridge.

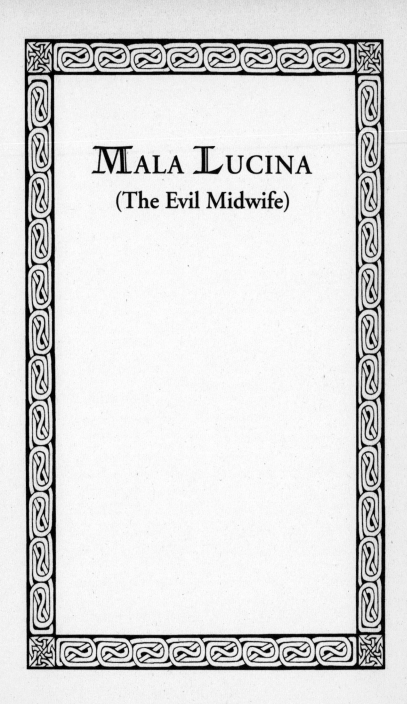

Mala Lucina

(The Evil Midwife)

The moon floats on fading daylight. The goddess Pressine traces carvings on the covering stone of a spring in the fecund wilderness of Poitou. Summer's end is near. Pressine wriggles her toes in moss, gaze fixed on a moonbeam only she can see.

The ground trembles. The covering stone shivers. A figure rides hard out of the distance. A large, hairy man on a red pony. His curly hair and beard are scarlet as sunset. His skin, where it is not tattooed in Pictish blue or covered with dust from his frantic gallop, is ruddy and freckled. He could pass for a god, but Pressine knows he is merely mortal.

He rushes past her, pulls his horse to a halt, wheels around and trots back. He stares like one who has just gained sight, looked at the moon for the first time and is stunned by its glamour.

"What ails you?" she snaps. She flips her ashen hair. She resents the intrusion.

"My name is Elinas. I am being pursued by a band of brigands, but I would die to know you."

"I am Pressine," she replies. She stands and raises her hands toward the horizon exactly as seven hostile horsemen appear.

Humming a high-pitched, unearthly tune and shooting lightning from her fingers, Pressine reduces the horsemen to gravel.

Then she returns to her seat by the well, where she struggles to bring her mind back to its pleasant emptiness, back to the moon.

Elinas will not leave. Pressine bites her pale lip and tries to ignore him, but he drops to his knees, lays his head in her lap and will give her no peace. He begs her to marry him.

Earth's shadow crosses the moon. Inch by inch, Elinas's persistence wears Pressine down, drags her into him like a tide. He is, after all, almost as vital as a god. At last, weakened and slightly giddy, Pressine agrees to marry Elinas on these conditions:

He must never, ever try to discover who she is or where she comes from. He must never, ever disrupt her solitude, or interfere with her moods, which obey the moon's commands and cannot be altered.

Elinas promises. He swears on stacks of holy stones and puddles of holy water that he will give Pressine her privacy and anything else she wants. She mounts his pony and leaves her home and all her sister goddesses and travels north with him to the gloaming, foggy highlands where he is a chieftain. There he builds a castle by a spring. Rain or shine, full or new, she contemplates the moon and sips from the spring, the source of life, the cradle of ebb and flow, the course of breath and becoming.

Sometimes Pressine is buoyant and festive. Sometimes she's shy, peeping incredulously at the world as if from behind clouds. Sometimes she gleams like a prism, ringed by a rainbow. Sometimes she feels as if she were shrinking, as if slivers of herself had been divided and greedily consumed. Sometimes she is dark, cold, cruel and invisible. She waxes and she wanes, mercurial yet predictable, and Elinas never, ever questions or reprimands her.

Pressine urinates only at night, and wherever she squats, a freshet, creek, stream, or river appears. So they live, more or less contentedly, in growing prosperity and abundance.

Until Pressine gives birth to three daughters.

Now his moon goddess has others to adore, so that Elinas's own adoration seems thin and paltry. She has daughters to fuss over and lullaby and nurse and instruct by the covering stone of the fountain. Now, when her glow fills Elinas with desire, he perceives her distractions, her lack of yearning for him absolutely.

The first small inquiries begin with the birth of Meliot, a child as crystalline and silvery and transparent as her mother. Elinas does not realize that he is seeking clues about Pressine's past. She is preoccupied and pays him no mind.

With the birth of Palatine, a child as plump and gold and amber as autumn, Elinas shifts from hints to crafty insinuation mingled with artful badgering. Still Pressine ignores him. She babies her babies, but the more she does, the more babying Elinas demands.

At night, musing alone by the covering stone of her fountain, Pressine wonders why she married him.

None of her sisters will marry. Human marriage, they say, makes a single mortal dependent upon another, a tyrannical oneness that casts aside the gods, marks other creatures as outsiders and creates a wedge between the Earth and her offspring.

The youngest daughter, Melusine, is a long, limber child, skin and hair as red as her father's. Her eyes are like the orbs of a bird and unblinking as a serpent's. Her mouth is wide, as if she could swallow the world whole. With her birth, Elinas drops all pretense. He bullies Pressine outright and constantly. "Tell me where you come from," he demands. "Who is your father? Who is your mother? Who do you meet when you leave my bed at night?"

Why did she not listen to her sisters? A union between mortal and deity, they cautioned, produces dire consequences, for humans are compelled to define, possess and control. Mortals believe themselves above the mysteries. They remake the mysteries to fit their own superstitions and ambitions. They have no faith in Nature.

Elinas nags on and on. "What do you do at night by the fountain when I am soundly sleeping? Who did you love before I found you?"

And the more he cajoles, the more he threatens, the more his vigorous redness fades to gloomy gray. The highland crops begin to fail. The wildflowers wither. Birdsongs cease. The grasses turn brown. The rivers dry. Cow udders shrink. Chickens no longer lay. Huntsmen complain of dwindling game. Children whimper with hunger.

"Enough!" Pressine screams. She curses him and swears her descendants will avenge her.

Elinas does not seem to hear. "Please tell me," he whines. "I love you. I must know everything about you."

Pressine raises her arms and gathers her daughters under the voluminous folds of her black cloak. The boom of a nighthawk's spreading wings within their bedchamber startles Elinas. When the bird is gone, Pressine and her daughters are gone as well.

174

Pressine flies to the Blessed Isle of Women, where she is welcomed by her sister goddesses. And briefly chastised.

Meliot, Palatine and Melusine thrive on the Blessed Isle, shrouded by goddesses, green mists and eternal loveliness. Each day is pretty and untroubled. But now their mother's lullabies are bitter verses about their father, satires that fuel their memory of him. They no longer recall whether Elinas had ever been a kindly or playful papa, whether he had loved them or ever looked on them with pride.

Yet they grow strong. They laugh and shout up and down the hills, in verdant woods and on velvet meadows. They run with deer and swim with dolphins. They sing with meadowlarks and nightingales. They take their daily lessons beside cool spring waters. Like all wise children, they are wary of their mother, but they are not afraid of Pressine. And soon each comes into her own moon time.

One morning—when they are long past lullabies but not the recollection of them—the three maidens stroll under the gentle sun of the Blessed Isle, and Melusine proposes a scheme to Palatine and Meliot that she is sure will please their mother.

That night, Elinas awakens, his graying mind trapped in a perpetual dream of Pressine.

The moon is dark, yet he sees her, surrounded by glittering rainbows. He leaves his chilly bed. He follows her out of the great hall of his castle, past the dessicated fountain, through the sterile fields, into the barren hills. He follows her along a path toward the high, high mountains. He follows her until his old, mortal legs ache.

He calls to the vision to stop. At the sound of her name, the image of Pressine evaporates into fog.

Meliot—whose skin and hair can catch and toss and shape all colors of light—signals her sister. Plump, golden Palatine sucks her breath and balloons into comforting hugeness. Warm and amber as a hearth, she looms over her father's bent back.

Elinas moans, head cushioned in his hands. Slowly, slowly, a round, soft gleam envelops and consoles him. He sees Pressine gliding up the mountain path. Voluptuous shadows roll from side to side as she beckons him.

Again he follows. Pleading, stumbling, lurching up and up and up, until he trips and falls face forward on the path. "Pressine," he mutters, "let me lay my head in your lap. Pressine."

At the sound of her name, the harvest moon folds and shrinks. Palatine stands on the path, hidden by night. She signals her sister.

Long, limber red Melusine exhales cold, dense clouds tough as tree limbs which curl around Elinas's shoulders and belly and knees and draw him to his feet. This tempestuous specter of Pressine thrills him. Again, he follows. Up and up and up. Until his daughters have lured him deep, deep into the high, high mountains.

There Meliot, Palatine and Melusine leave their father to wander forever in the crags and crannies of rocks and stones, far from springs or fountains. The relentless mountain moon blazes like the desert sun, and blinds Elinas.

Meliot, Palatine and Melusine return to the Blessed Isle. Chattering, giggling, twittering, they tell their mother of their adventure.

Pressine is furious.

"How dare you do such a thing without consulting me!" she shrills. "How dare you take revenge by glamouring him with my images and *leave me out*!

"You presumptuous wretches! You miserable, ungrateful, disloyal progeny!"

"Disloyal? But Mother," Meliot protests, "did you not say that your descendants would take revenge on our father? Are we not your descendants?"

"Not without my counsel! Not without my direction! Not without my instructions! It was an offense he committed against me—*me*!"

She raises her hands and points at her eldest daughter. Spiderwebs shoot from her fingers and wrap Meliot round and round. The girl gasps for air. She closes her eyes. When she opens them again, she is alone in a granite palace and the thick web that had bound her now blocks the entrances. Meliot's silver light dulls to pewter.

"Oh, Mother," Palatine pleads. "We did it for you. We thought you'd be pleased. We did our best—"

"Best?!" Pressine yells. "Best me no bests! What do you know about best when it comes to mortals? Think you because you have traces of Earth in your gold hair and fat, fertile flesh that you know humans? How dare you steal my magnetism to entice him? Best? I—not you—know best!"

She raises her hands and points at her middle daughter. Sticky milk splashes from Palatine's breasts onto her feet. She stares at the floor as milk rises above her ankles. When she lifts her eyes, she finds herself in the high, high mountains with her father, doomed to guide him through the sharp crags and crannies of stones and rock and quench his terrible thirst at her teats.

Melusine writhes and flicks her tongue around her lips.

Pressine growls. "You, little ringleader, will also leave the Blessed Isle. Once a month for three days, you will become a snake up to the waist. Worst of all, you will marry a mortal."

Melusine sighs and twists her long, limber legs.

"And be happy," Pressine adds, menacingly.

"Think you this will be easy? You must hide and guard your snake aspect. When you marry, you must keep this a secret always from your husband."

Melusine watches Pressine, unblinking, uncomprehending.

"Yours is the harshest punishment. You will, in your own way, repeat my mistakes." And Pressine aims her thin, shivering fingers at her youngest daughter.

Melusine finds herself by a dusty fountain in a hot and dirty town. No trees. No meadows. No refreshing breezes. Spindly weeds struggle through cracks in stone paving. Grimy buildings, shacks and mansions crowd one another. Sallow, sickly humans slog through piles of garbage, oblivious to the flies and stink. Beggars and princes and merchants, hurrying, shoving. Snarling at children, kicking dogs, whipping horses, slaughtering birds and animals. Here in Poitou, there is no longer a trace of Pressine's fecund wilderness and few remember her, except in legend. They have named her Mala Lucina, Evil Midwife, and blame her for the birth of their misfortunes.

Melusine weeps. She rubs her eyes with her scarlet hair. If her mother loathes her enough to curse her and exile her to this unwholesome place, then she must be worth despising. She will accept her punishment, uncomplaining. On Pressine's behalf, Melusine resolves never to forgive herself.

Will she be allowed to return home? Will she see her sisters again? What will become of her in the meantime? Which of these awful mortals might shelter her in which of their close and lightless hovels? But no one notices the long, limber red beauty, who sobs, unblinking, on the covering stone of the foul city fountain.

Until a young man comes running toward her. He waves a sword and shouts over his shoulder.

Raimond de Lusignan catches a glimpse of Melusine as he speeds by. He heels and turns back. Seven angry attackers approach, but he cannot move. Not even to save his own life.

"Why are you crying?" he asks Melusine. "Who are you?" The attackers aim their axes at the nape of Raimond's neck.

Melusine gasps. "Behind you!" she cries.

And it is said in Poitou that a huge crimson serpent appeared where a maiden had been, and wrapped itself around all seven angry attackers at once and crushed them all at once to death.

Raimond sees no fearsome serpent. He sees only a beautiful girl sobbing at the fountain. He has forgotten entirely about the attackers. He is engulfed in Melusine. In her bird eyes. Her scarlet hair. Her massive mouth. Smiling, Raimond helps to wipe her tears with his own dark curls. Then he kisses her and takes her hand and begs her to be his wife.

She agrees without hesitation. Her mother has cursed her to marry a mortal. No one, not even a demigoddess, can avoid a mother's curse.

But as they walk hand in hand toward his castle, Melusine remembers. "I'll go no farther with you," she says, "until and unless you swear that you will never, ever try to discover who I am or where I go once a month for three days."

Raimond does not swear on stacks of holy stones or puddles of holy water. Those disappeared with the wilderness, when Pressine eloped with a mortal chieftain. Instead, Raimond simply promises not to pry. There is such earnestness in his dark eyes that Melusine is overcome with trust and joy and desire. In that moment, she forgets her exile.

He lays her on his bed. She wraps her long and limber legs around his back and flicks her tongue on his. Raimond slides into Melusine. And they are happy.

Happy for ten years and ten exceptional sons.

But each month, when the moon is full, Pressine's voice penetrates Melusine's skull. She becomes shy and nervous. Her head aches. Her skin itches. Her belly cramps. Her thighs twitch. Slower and slower she moves about her rooms and gardens.

Until the flesh below her waist begins to expand and melt together.

She slips unseen through a door in the castle floor. She waddles quickly, down and down steep, steep steps. She wriggles and she ripples through a narrow passage, down and down far below the Earth. Below the sea.

Until she reaches a spring in a deep, deep cave.

Her unblinking eyes glaze. She undulates between stalagmites, scraping her scales. She sloughs her skin. She sucks her thick crimson tail. Coiled in a circle, time stops.

Her thoughts spin into a tight, impenetrable ball of self-loathing and nostalgia. She hisses. She spits. She berates herself and argues ferociously with her reflection in the spring. Mimicking her mother's voice, speaking unspeakable cruelties. Sometimes the pathetic vision of her father, ruddy and reminiscent of herself, swims across her mirrored face. Sometimes she sobs for her sisters. Sometimes she chews her tail until the blood runs.

Meanwhile, the world about her flourishes. Month by month, with each of Melusine's absences, Earth's wounds begin to heal. Clear water flows into the city fountain. Cool rain cleanses the dusty city. The fields grow fertile. Green wilderness is restored, and with it the holy stones and holy waters. Wild beasts and birds multiply. Poitou floods with abundance and harmony that was lost when Pressine left.

Some mortals feel their faith in Nature revitalized. They

regret their greed and recall how once they had lived in balance with the swift moods of the moon and the creeping changes of the Earth.

But others drone: "Mala Lucina has come back. This goodness cannot last. Disaster awaits us. We must prepare for betrayal."

Raimond pretends not to notice Melusine's bloodied feet when she returns, relieved and cheerful from her monthly journey, unaware that it is her transformation and her essence that succors bounty.

Raimond loves Melusine with the potent yearning of a new and young lover. Neither grows older. Passion nourishes and suspends them. Each day, they slough the skin of petty resentments. Raimond keeps his promise. He speaks no harsh or curious word about her absences. He turns a deaf ear to frightening rumors. He never questions Melusine about her origins, even as each son is born bearing a strange and supernatural mark.

The first has a third eye in the middle of his forehead. Another has fangs that graze his jaw. Still another's toes are webbed. Another's ears are jugged. Another has white eyes. Another has tiny wings. Another, a small and wormish tail.

The fearful sibilations increase. "Evil Midwife! Mala Lucina!" By the birth of the tenth son—whose back is hunched and fluted and armored like a lizard's—most mortals of Poitou have forgotten their good fortune. Prophets warn of pestilence and famine. The people pillage the wilderness and slaughter wild beasts and birds to hoard against time. Melusine's ten sons, they say, are wicked portents of Nature's unpredictability, and they must take control against the inevitable.

Whispers become shouts. Wherever Raimond goes, stories of Mala Lucina pursue him. "None who midwife can be evil," he says, "for they serve the renewal of life. It is your pillaging and hoarding that will destroy us. Can you not see the forest for the trees?"

His ministers beg Raimond to dispose of his wife. "Where does she truly come from?" they ask. "Who is she really? She is not one of us. Sooner or later, she will bring destruction."

Outside the castle, crowds dance in mocking ripples and spirals. They chant, "Mala Lucina! Spare us! Have mercy upon us!"

Raimond watches the hideous carnival from a window. Behind him, he hears the door close quietly in the floor as Melusine departs on her monthly retreat. He waits. The crowd burns poppets and effigies. Some wear dragon and viper masks. Others are painted and costumed with the birthmarks of Raimond's beloved sons, these boys who bridge the gap between Earth and her offspring.

He tiptoes to the door in the floor. He squeezes through it, and down and down he stumbles. Down steep, steep steps. Far below the Earth. Below the sea.

Until he comes to a cave, where a faint light glimmers.

He hides in the shadows. He sees Melusine's sausage tail. He sees her red scales. The piles of skin she sheds month after month. He sees the fecund life that grows from her excrement, even in the dark of the den. He watches her slither and he sees her slide. He sees the long, winding track she leaves in the dirt. He sees her climb into her green marble bath, the serpent's egg from which time is born and born again. He watches her shove her tail into her wide, wide mouth. He watches the bathwater rise red around her breasts.

Her eyes glaze. He perceives the dream she dreams of Pressine. He feels her anger and poisonous self-loathing.

Melusine sniffs the air. She hisses. She spits. She turns her head. Round and round.

Until her eyes meet Raimond's.

She screams, "No! Mother! No!"

Her neck stretches and curves. She sprouts red wattles. Her mouth narrows and takes the form of a beak. Her nose and forehead elongate and black and gray feathers grow on the face that has become a crane's. She stretches her arms to Raimond and they turn to wings.

With another anguished cry, she flies away.

She flies toward the Blessed Isle of Women, drawn by the full moon. By Pressine's voice that grows louder and louder as the moon rises closer and closer. Melusine's heart pounds. She will soon be with her mother. She will soon be reunited with her sisters. Faster and faster she flies.

Until two silver clouds slip across the sky. Meliot and Palatine obscure the scowling face of the moon. Melusine hovers. Meliot and Palatine sway across the light of the moon, whispering.

In that moment, in that forgiving, sisterly darkness, Melusine understands who she is and that without her, the world she has left and her ten sons will perish.

She swoops and circles. Away from the moon. Away from the Blessed Isle. She pumps her great white wings. She flies faster and faster back to Poitou. She will not repeat her mother's mistakes. She will refuse her mother's curse. Yet by defying Pressine, she knows she can never, ever return as she was.

It is said in Poitou that Melusine never again saw Raimond, but each night, she returned to human form to suckle her sons. By day she sleeps curled on the warm covering stone of a fountain and guards the land. Despite the determination of mortals to destroy themselves, despite their fear of her and her kind and their cries of "Mala Lucina!" she protects, unblinking, what she can. She rules by flexibility, not mood. She does not hide. She continues to renew and regenerate, to midwife knowledge and give birth to time, time and time again. No longer does she bleed, but the serpent tracks she leaves in the dirt form rivers, streams, freshets and creeks.

One night, when the moon is a bright, sharp sickle, the mortals of Poitou hear a great whooping and frantic flapping of wings. A crane balances on the castle ramparts twisting its long, limber neck and shaking its red wattles and wailing.

Raimond de Lusignan has grown old and died.

Retold from a tale of Brittany.

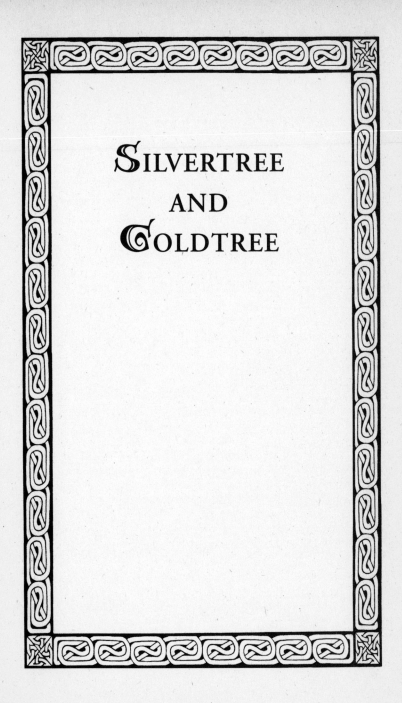

SILVERTREE
AND
GOLDTREE

O nce upon a time, there was a queen named Silvertree and the name of her daughter was Goldtree.

One day, Silvertree took Goldtree to a glen, where there was a well in which there was a trout. A magic, talking trout, an informed trout, a trout no one dared to eat, and you will soon see why. Silvertree beckoned Goldtree to crouch beside her. She spread her gown across the flagstone, leaned into the well, smiling confidently and radiantly into the water.

"Troutie, bonnie little fellow," she called, "am I not the most beautiful woman in the world?"

The trout was questioned by Silvertree annually. His answer had always been satisfactory. So satisfactory it dulled his imagination to repeat it year after year, but like all trout, he was compelled to be honest.

"No, indeed," he burbled, "you are not."

Silvertree's eyes widened, her faint crow's-feet darkened, and her mouth grew tense, exaggerating the little lines above her lips. "And if I am not the most beautiful woman in the world," she sniffed, "who is?"

"Why, Goldtree, of course," the trout said. "Your own growing daughter. And you should be proud to have mothered such a one."

Maternal pride was the furthest thing from Silvertree's mind. She stood indignantly, glowered at Goldtree and marched away from the glen, leaving her befuddled daughter to make her own way home. And this, it must be added, took the girl some time to do. Although she was at the peak of youthful blush and bloom, Goldtree's brains had not yet blossomed.

Silvertree muttered to herself as she stormed up the castle steps. "Not until I am dead and gone is Goldtree to take my place as the most beautiful woman in the world, and maybe not even then," she mumbled, and slammed the door to her chamber.

Then she collapsed on her bed in tears and rage.

"That fish has made me ill," she told her maid, "and I will not recover until I have the heart and liver of Goldtree to eat."

The maid tucked her mistress under the covers and ran home to embrace her own daughter and whisper generous loving words in the little girl's ear and wonder at the privilege of royalty.

At nightfall, when the king returned from inspecting his lands and performing the necessary imperial pillaging, he was told that his cherished wife was ill and that she might not survive. He hurried to her chamber and found Silvertree wan and weeping into a mountain of satin pillows.

Silvertree glared bitterly at her husband and rejected his solicitations. He was miserable when his wife was not content. For the truth was, though Silvertree had reached her middle years and, by the relentless standards of bards, portrait painters and fashion designers, had to concede her beauty to younger women, she was still exquisite and the king still found her irresistible. Should she live through this dreadful blow, she would, she determined, have all the bards, portrait painters and fashion designers in the kingdom put to death.

"You could heal my illness if you truly desire," she sobbed, while the king shifted his considerable weight from toe to toe.

"Anything at all, my love," he promised. "Say what you need and I will provide it."

"In that case," Silvertree said, "I'll be cured if you give me the heart and liver of Goldtree to eat."

The king's nervous shuffle froze for just an instant. He did not reply. He patted his wife's plump paps, then left the room and left her to rest.

As it happened, a prince from across the sea had been asking the king for Goldtree's hand. The prince was persistent, but the king had been pondering the match at his leisure. Now he readily agreed. That very afternoon, he sent Goldtree across the sea to the prince with a large dowry to ensure the longevity of the marriage.

Then he called his huntsmen and ordered them to the hunting hill to kill a billy goat.

As you will recall from other stories of this nature, the huntsmen delivered the heart and liver of the goat to the king, who had them roasted in delicate sauces he considered worthy of a princess's gizzards, and then served the disguised dishes himself to Silvertree piping hot on a tray.

The queen ate carefully and prayerfully, glancing with each bite at herself in a mirror across the room. Indeed, she seemed to grow younger as she ate. She licked and picked lovingly at her food and savored every morsel. Perhaps because these were the innards of a billy goat, her meal did not conjure up regret and fond memories of Goldtree's birth, her darling infancy, her sweet toddling, her first halting words, the day she cut her fore-head and ran to her mother for comfort. . . .

When the plate was clean, Silvertree rose from her sickbed, strong and healthy.

The king enjoyed many fine favors from his wife. Each day, Silvertree awoke singing, and each night she slept like a baby, for deep sleep smooths the wrinkling brow.

And after a restful year, she returned to the glen where there was a well in which there was a trout.

"Troutie, bonnie fellow," she said, peering into the mossy water, "am I not the most beautiful woman in the world?"

"Indeed," the trout sputtered succinctly, "you are not."

Silvertree gripped the edge of the well and her lip quivered.

"If not me," she said, suppressing a scream, "then who?"

"Why, Goldtree, your daughter. And you should be proud to have mothered such a one."

"Goldtree is dead, troutie. I have consumed her beauty. It must be she you see in me."

"Goldtree is not dead. She is married to a great prince who lives across the sea."

That night, Silvertree refused to let the king enter her chamber. She double-bolted the door and stationed her maid outside to guard it.

The king whined through the door for Silvertree to reveal why she'd withdrawn her favors. Behind his back, the maid rolled her eyes and wondered at the privilege of royalty.

"I want to see Goldtree in her new kingdom," Silvertree shouted at the king. The sound of a heavy diamond bracelet smashing against granite followed. "It has been a year since I laid eyes on my own precious daughter. Give me a ship so I may go."

The king caught his breath. How can we know what he thought? Much to the frustration of their wives and daughters—not to speak of the peasantry—kings keep their thoughts to themselves. Perhaps he hoped this request meant remorse and a reconciliation. He agreed to give Silvertree his longship, while she, in turn, agreed to let him enter her chamber and welcomed him wearing diaphanous silk.

Silvertree guided the longship herself, and she steered it so well the journey was quick and smooth.

Goldtree peered out her castle window. Her veil whipped about her face, and at first she thought she saw a mirage. Upon securing the frolicking mantle, she realized this was no sea vision but her father's longship skimming the water toward shore. And she knew what that meant. How did she know? Anyone with a mother can intuit that mother's imminent arrival.

The prince, of course, was away hunting. Goldtree rushed down the winding tower stairs, shrieking for her servants. "Oh see, oh see, oh say can you see that longship?" she cried. "My mother navigates it and she is coming to kill me!"

As Silvertree anchored the ship, the servants locked Goldtree in a room, hid the key, then retreated to the kitchen to wonder at the privilege of royalty.

Silvertree swept into the great hall of the castle. "Daughter! Come greet your own loving mother when she visits you," she called through the drafty rooms.

At last, a timid voice piped up from behind an iron door. "I cannot, Mama. I am locked in this room and can't get out."

"What a crummy husband," Silvertree grumbled to herself, and then aloud to Goldtree she said, "Darling girl, can you not at least stick your finger through the keyhole so that I can kiss it?"

Goldtree's heart pounded with fear and love as she stuck her pinkie through the keyhole.

Silvertree pulled a dagger from her cape. She held Goldtree's finger steady and stabbed it with the poisoned tip.

"Oh, Mama, what stinging lips you have," Goldtree croaked, and fell dead on the floor behind the door.

Then Silvertree boarded the longship and returned home.

As beautiful as she'd been in life, Goldtree was more so now, and the prince could not bring himself to bury her. He laid her on a white marble slab, encased in a glass coffin, and locked the room where she had died. No one was permitted in the chamber, but the prince wept daily over Goldtree's remains, while the servants wondered at the privilege of royalty.

Two seasons passed, and the prince began to feel lonely. What's more, his house was in terrible disarray. He took a new wife.

His second queen, like Silvertree, was a woman "of a certain age." She did not have Goldtree's elastic beauty, nor did she want it. She was elegant and handsome, mirthful, bright and serene. She did not need a fish to tell her who she was. She was pleased with the wise gray strands in her hair. Despite the fine lines on her brow and around her mouth and eyes, everyone who met her loved her, a fact that made bards, portrait painters and fashion designers uneasy.

She carried the keys to each room of the castle on a copper belt around her waist, and she ruled the household with a firm and gentle hand.

But there was one key the prince would not give his new wife. She was curious about the room no one was allowed to enter, but she left well enough alone.

Until one day, on the anniversary of Goldtree's death, the prince left the castle to pursue an imperial adventure and, in his sadness and haste, forgot the key.

His new wife found it beside their bed. She fondled it and

inspected it closely and carefully. She considered the great risk of opening the door. Then she shrugged and entered the forbidden room.

We know what she found. And she was dazzled. "Oh, poor thing," she said. "You are the most beautiful woman in the world. What a shame."

She circled Goldtree's glass coffin until she discovered hinges. She raised it and set it aside. She shook and turned and pinched the dead woman. All to no avail, until she glanced down at Goldtree's pinkie and noticed swelling and a welt of dried blood.

"Och," said the new wife and dropped to her knees. She lifted the stiff pinkie to her lips. With one sudden kiss, she sucked up the poison and spit it out. Goldtree rose, alive, refreshed and grinning.

The prince's adventures had yielded him nothing. His heart had not been in the task. He returned home that night downcast and forlorn.

His new wife approached him with a merry glitter in her eyes. "What gift would you give me," she asked, "if I could make you laugh? Would you return my dowry and give me my freedom?"

The prince moped. Sulkily, he replied, "You may have anything you want, wife. On such a day as this, I think only of Goldtree. Nothing would make me laugh but that she come alive again."

The new wife chuckled and clinked the keys at her waist. "Go to your forbidden room and you will find your Goldtree alive and well."

The prince did not believe her. He stared viciously into his mead bowl. The new wife took him by the hand and led him down the hallway. He kicked the half-opened door to the forbidden room, imagining how he would punish his new wife for her disobedience. But to his astonishment, there was Goldtree sitting on her marble slab. He yelped for joy, grabbed her and kissed her and tickled her and made love to her on the marble slab, across the hump of the glass coffin and on the floor.

Afterward, the prince and his two wives shared a hardy supper.

"I have restored your first wife," the second wife said to the prince. "I will accept my gifts now and depart, for I have other plans."

"Oh, no!" the prince and Goldtree cried. "You must not leave."

"I would be content with two wives," said the prince. "Especially such a pair as you."

The new wife shook her head, no.

"Stay a little while," Goldtree pleaded. "The life of a first wife is lonely, especially if she is the most beautiful woman in the world, whose mother yearns for her death."

"Indeed, that would be embarrassing," the new wife said, and consented.

Meanwhile, Silvertree went to the glen where there was a well in which there was a trout. "Troutie, bonnie little fellow," she giggled, "am I not the most beautiful woman in the world?"

"Indeed, you are not," the trout sighed.

"Who is it now, for heaven's sake! This is really exasperating, troutie!"

"Why, it's Goldtree, your own daughter, and you should be proud to have mothered such a one."

"Nonsense!" Silvertree yelled. The trout slid deeper into the well. "Listen to me, you slimy little shit! I'll serve you up with almondine sauce! Goldtree is not alive. I killed her a year ago with my poisoned dagger!"

"Och, but she did not die," the trout said, and disappeared forever.

Again, Silvertree insisted that the king give her his longship. Again, he agreed. She sped across the sea, navigating straight and fast, and no one else was permitted to handle the helm.

Goldtree and the new wife peered out the castle window. The prince, as usual, was away hunting.

"Look! Look!" Goldtree pointed and jabbed hysterically at the air. "There is my father's longship. My mother has come to kill me again."

"Piffle," answered the new wife. She took Goldtree's hand. "Let's go down to meet her."

Goldtree shuddered. Her teeth rattled. Her heart thumped. Thanks to the privilege of royalty, she was not permitted to crack her knuckles or pick her nose, but she wanted to.

"Goldtree, my love, my darling child, come and greet your own dear mother. Share with me this cup of wine," Silvertree pleaded.

As Goldtree reached for the cup, her hands shaking, the second wife stepped between them.

"It is the custom of this country," she told Silvertree, "that the person who offers a drink takes a draft of it first."

Silvertree put the cup to her mouth. The second wife struck the cup with the heel of her hand so that some of the drink spilled into the queen's throat. Silvertree dropped dead. Goldtree gasped in horror and relief. She was not really sure which she felt, if either.

Then the new wife ordered a deep grave to be dug and

Silvertree to be buried facedown within it, so she could never rise again.

"Oh, dear," said Goldtree. "I may miss my mama, after all. But at least I have you," she said.

The new wife shook her head, no.

"Where will you go? How will you live without a palace and a prince and the privilege of royalty?" Goldtree asked.

The new wife laughed. "That won't be hard," she said. "In fact, it will be much easier. Mind you, wherever I go, I'll have no truck with trout, magic or otherwise. I advise you to do the same, my dear."

Goldtree smiled nicely.

The second wife gathered her dowry and mounted her palfrey. She kissed Goldtree and hoped for the best.

Retold from a Scottish faery tale.

THE CAILLEACH

(Old Woman)

Wherever he went, the Daghda transported his cock in a cart. He pushed the barrow along the flat plain. There were no rivers. No hills. No valleys. No mountains. No women. One day, the Daghda, father-chieftain of the people of the goddess, the Tuatha De Danann, had a dream.

He dreamed of cunts. His member unfurled. Cunts here. It swelled. Cunts there. It dilated. Cunts everywhere. His cock thickened and lengthened so that the Daghda could not reach the cart with his hands. The cart stopped. He kicked it. Fell on it. The cart would not budge.

The Daghda dismounted his cock in order to pull the cart. The eye of his cock lodged in the ground. Lifted the Daghda. He dangled, suspended high on his organ. He kicked and flailed, then vaulted back to his feet. He gave the cart a mighty shove. It tipped on its side. The wheel, spinning, had accidentally excavated the slit of the Daghda's dreams.

Warm and sticky mud. Spongy, fleshy clay. The Daghda plunged right in. Enjoyed himself all day. Drank liquor from his leather pouch. He humped. He sang. He pumped. Drank some more. Sang some more. Bumped some more. Again and again and again.

The Daghda collapsed. He sighed. Kissed the sky. Uprighted

himself. Uprighted his cart. He patted his prick. He went along his blissful way.

The moon was fat and diaphanous. The Earth trembled and shook. The Earth labored. The Earth expelled a giant female. Bald head. Bald mound. Pendulous paps. Drumlin haunches. Hammock bum. She jetted out of the womb-on-the-wasteland, into the sky. In her cunt, the Cailleach carried stones, rocks, boulders, pebbles of every color, twist and size. She hurled far above the Earth. She rested on a cloud knoll.

The Daghda slept. Cock curled round him for a blanket. Balls a beefy pillow. The sun rose. The Cailleach watched the Daghda toss his cock in his cart. Watched him whistle across the flat plain.

The Daghda spied a wee, damp fissure, a fountain in a field. Recalled his previous pleasure. His member bulged. Broadened and blossomed. He deployed it in the spring. Cool and moist and flowing. Tight enough to give his pulsing pecker purchase. He humped. He doused. He pumped. He bumped.

The Cailleach watched. Her pudenda pounded. She howled desire. Whimpered and whined excitement. Clutched her clitoris. Fingered her labia. Unfolded her inner lips. Stones, pebbles, rocks, boulders tumbled from her cunt. Obsidian and tuff. Sandstone and limestone. Chalk and quartz. Shale, basalt. Gneiss. They spread across the firmament and over the channel. Wherever they landed, mountains, highlands, islands, cairns and lake beds formed. The Cailleach grinned a half-grin. Drowsy satisfaction.

The Daghda thrust at the spring. A bubbling cry of protest! A female spirit surged from the pussy-in-the-pasture. Boane gripped the Daghda's cock. Flung it aside. Indignant. The force of its landing caused the crack in the meadow to quake open. A flood burst from the vaporous vagina. Burst across the plain.

Filled the dry lake beds. Irrigated the dust. The Earth sprouted green and green and green again. From crust to soil. Mold and humus. Loam and sod. Grasses and sedges and rushes. Shrubs. Trees. Gorse and heather. Bracken and moss. Wormy, spermy creatures.

Boane whacked the Daghda's cock with a rock. Retreat. Too late. In nine months' time, the spring gave birth to Oenghus, whose only thoughts were ever of love. Who wore the white swan's wings.

Angry Boane dilated into a torrent. Splayed and coalesced into a river that crashed to the sea. Estuaries gushed from her confluent cunt. Dust eroded to silt. Fishes and kelp. Neap tides and undertow. She made gulfs. She cut streams and creeks. Her fluids carved reefs. The spirit's waters granulated sediment. She sliced cliffs and crags. Peninsulas.

The Daghda pushed on, seeking the cunts of his dream. Cunts of every color, twist and size. In hollows. In caves. In wells and tunnels, shafts and pits. Tectonic twats. Dimples on the green. He wandered along his horny way, cock in cart, and wherever he went, he spread his seed. Men and women sprang out of rocks and dirt. Up from ponds and brooks.

The Cailleach spins round and round the sky. She blights growth when the sun shrinks small in fall. Turns to stone. Erect. Alone. Till winter's end. She takes ripe husbands in May when the sun is big. The Cailleach has had seven thousand husbands, one for every year. They age and die. The Cailleach grows old. Then young and green again and again and again green. Seven thousand times.

The Daghda stumps up lumpy hills and down stark peaks. Highland, lowland. Forest and pool, heath and bog. When he crosses the river Boyne, Boane rages and spits. She snatches at the Daghda's loins and tries to drown him.

The Daghda dreams on. Drinks liquor from his leather pouch and sings. Seeking cunts. Cunts there. Cunts here. Cunts anywhere. Pushing his barrow. Petting his precious, protruding cargo.

A BRIEF PRONUNCIATION GUIDE

Morrigna	—	Mor-rig-nuh
Macha	—	Mah-ha
Crunnchu	—	Croon-hoo
Samhain	—	Sah-wain
Medb	—	Maeve
Pwyll	—	Powell
CuChulainn	—	Coo-hul-en
Scatach	—	Ska-tah
Blodeuwedd	—	Blood-wed
Lugh, Llew	—	Loo
Criedne	—	Crej-nuh
Aoife	—	A-fuh
Fionn mac Cumhal	—	Finn mac Cool
Tuiren	—	Toor-un
Muirne	—	Mwir-nuh
Uchtdealb	—	Ukt-jelb
Fionnlaith	—	Finlay
Sadb	—	Sav
Fear Doirche	—	Fair Door-huh
Niamh	—	Nee-ev
Oisin	—	Oo-sheen
Daire Mor	—	Dar-uh More
Dubh Ruis	—	Duv Rush
Cailleach	—	Cal-yach

Ⓟ **PLUME**   Ⓜ **MERIDIAN**

ESSAY COLLECTIONS

☐ **CONCEIVED WITH MALICE** *Literature as Revenge in the Lives and Works of Virginia and Leonard Woolf, D.H. Lawrence, Djuna Barnes, and Henry Miller* **by Louise De Salvo.** Full of enticing literary gossip, the author vividly describes how these great literary figures each perceived an attack on the self—and struck back through their art, creating lasting monuments to their deepest hurts and darkest obsessions. "Delicious, intelligent, irresistible, one of the darker pleasures."—Carole Maso, author of *The American Woman in the Chinese Hat*   (273234—$13.95)

☐ **WRITING THE SOUTHWEST by David King Dunaway.** The common thread that links such writers as Edward Abbey, Tony Hillerman, Joy Harjo, Barbara Kingsolver, and Terry McMillan is an understanding of the interplay between humans and the earth. This compelling collection offers outstanding selections of contemporary southwestern literature along with a biographical profile, a bibliography, and an original interview with each of the 14 authors included.   (273943—$12.95)

☐ **DESIRE AND IMAGINATION** *Classic Essays in Sexuality.* **Edited by Regina Barreca, Ph.D.** While the 19th century has come to be thought of as an age of prudery and restraint, there was at that time a veritable explosion of research, study, and writing done on provocative subjects like female desire, erotic stimuli, homosexuality, and masturbation. These twenty rarely seen essays from writers like Martineau, Krafft-Ebing, Darwin Ellis, Sanger, and Freud illuminate the way in which we choose even today to define what is "normal" behavior and what is regarded with suspicion.   (011507—$13.95)

☐ **MASSACRE OF THE DREAMERS** *Essays on Xicanisma* **by Ana Castillo.** In this provocative collection of essays, award-winning poet, novelist, scholar, and activist/curandera Ana Castillo becomes a voice for Mexic Amerindian women silenced for hundreds of years by the dual censorship of being female and brown-skinned. She explores all aspects of their collective identity and aims to inform, raise consciousness, and incite Chicanas—and all caring people—to change mainstream society from one of exclusion to inclusion. "Castillo goes after our hearts and minds, not territory or power."—*Village Voice*   (274249—$11.95)

Prices slightly higher in Canada.

PL228

UNIQUE COLLECTIONS

☐ **THE BOOK OF LOVE *Writers and Their Love Letters*. Selected and Introduction by Cathy N. Davidson.** This entrancing collection of 100 intimate letters puts into unforgettable words all the meanings of love—from spiritual joy to erotic ecstasy, from deep fulfillment to painful heartbreak, from the thrill of falling in love to the ache of loss. The time span covered in this volume extends from the classical Greece of Sappho and the ancient Rome of Marcus Aurelius to the 20th-century Paris of Henry Miller and the America of John Cheever and Anne Sexton. "Adroitly edited . . . cleverly arranged . . . will elicit sighs—and sobs."—*New York Daily News*   (275946—$12.95)

☐ **THE MERIDIAN ANTHOLOGY OF 18th- AND 19th-CENTURY BRITISH DRAMA. Edited and with an Introduction by Katharine M. Rogers.** A collection of eight milestones in British drama that offers a rich theatrical perspective on two centuries in the artistic, cultural, political, and economic life of England: *The Beaux' Stratagem, The Conscious Lovers, The Beggar's Opera, The London Merchant, The School for Scandal, The Octoroon, Ruddigore,* and *The Importance of Being Earnest.*   (008484—$14.95)

☐ **THE MERIDIAN ANTHOLOGY OF RESTORATION AND EIGHTEENTH-CENTURY PLAYS BY WOMEN. Edited by Katharine M. Rogers.** The women represented in this groundbreaking anthology—the only collection of Restoration and eighteenth-century plays devoted exclusively to women—had but one thing in common: the desire to ignore convention and write for the stage. These women legitimized the profession for their sex.   (011108—$15.95)

☐ **THE MERIDIAN ANTHOLOGY OF EARLY WOMEN WRITERS *British Literary Women From Aphra Behn to Maria Edgeworth 1660–1800* edited by Katharine M. Rogers and William McCarthy.** Here are nineteen stunning pre-nineteenth-century female literary talents never before collected in a single volume. Their stories bring to light the rich heritage of early literary creativity among women.   (008484—$14.95)

Prices slightly higher in Canada.
